THE INTOLERANT INDIAN

Advance Praise for *The Intolerant Indian*

'... a deeply serious and controversial study by a skilled and very knowledgeable journalist... The book closely argues that there is a very real threat to Indian democracy from pervasive social inequalities, opposition to free expression of unpopular ideas, and, above all, from intolerance on the part of dominant religious groups... This is truly a tract for our perilous times that deserves a wide and careful readership.'

AINSLIE T. EMBREE, PROFESSOR EMERITUS OF HISTORY, COLUMBIA UNIVERSITY

'... eye-opening, thought-provoking and superbly written. While the title, for us as Indians, may be provocative, the book's message is uncontestable. It is simply that, as a nation, India is certainly liberal and secular, but as people we are often intolerant of diversity of religion, ideology or culture among different segments of society... Highly recommended, this book should in fact be compulsory reading for aspiring politicians as well as in colleges and universities.'

BIMAL JALAN, AUTHOR AND FORMER GOVERNOR, RESERVE BANK OF INDIA

This is a timely, topical and cogently written book on a critical and contested issue – the current state and the likely future of Indian secularism. Those with an interest in contemporary India will find this analysis illuminating, insightful and telling.

SUMIT GANGULY, RABINDRANATH TAGORE CHAIR IN INDIAN CULTURES AND CIVILIZATIONS, INDIANA UNIVERSITY, BLOOMINGTON

Gautam Adhikari spares no punches in a sharp attack on religious extremists of all kinds, and on organized religion itself, while insisting on the right of every citizen, including the extremist and the fundamentalist, to a free expression of views. This is an important book for all, especially for those Indians who may have taken the republic for granted.

KARAN THAPAR, TV JOURNALIST AND COLUMNIST

THE INTOLERANT INDIAN

WHY WE MUST REDISCOVER A LIBERAL SPACE

GAUTAM ADHIKARI

HarperCollins *Publishers* India

First published in India by
HarperCollins *Publishers* in 2011

Building 10, Tower A, 4th Floor, DLF Cyber City, Phase II,
Gurugram Haryana – 122002, India
www.harpercollins.co.in

2 4 6 8 10 9 7 5 3

P-ISBN: 978-93-5029-051-4
E-ISBN: 978-93-5029-529-8

Typeset in ITC Giovanni Std 11.5/15.5
InoSoft Systems

Printed and bound at
MicroPrints India, New Delhi

For Rita, Priya, Brinda, Saira,
Rohan, Jeffrey and Peter

CONTENTS

PREFACE

When the idea of writing this book came up in a conversation with my publisher, a suggestion for its proposed title was *Intolerant India.* We rejected that because the idea was not to portray India as an intolerant nation. No, I just wanted to talk about those of our compatriots who did not seem to appreciate the idea of pluralist tolerance, which formed the structural framework of Indian democracy. Hence the title *The Intolerant Indian*; this extended essay is about those Indians – alas, far too many – who see pluralism as phony and tolerant secularism as hypocritical or irrelevant to an existence revolving around narrow religious, regional or ethnic identities.

Liberal and secular pluralism forms a framework drawn from the principle of 'unity in diversity', which two of this nation's intellectual leaders, Mohandas Gandhi and Rabindranath Tagore, took as a starting point for the idea of India. To paraphrase Tagore from that well-known, oft-quoted and under-appreciated poem in the *Gitanjali,* it would be a place where a citizen's mind would be without fear and everyone would be able to hold their heads high; where knowledge would be freely gathered and exchanged; where society would not be broken up by narrow domestic walls of misunderstanding and hatred; and where the clear stream of reason would not lose its way in the dreary desert sands of habit or mindless tradition. That is what India was dreamt to be. That is why the founding fathers wrote a secular constitution; that is what India should be if it has to survive as the world's boldest experiment in democracy.

In the sixty years of its existence as an independent democratic republic, has India lived up to the dream? Yes, by and large, but not every citizen's mind is without fear and not everyone can hold their heads high. That is because walls of hateful intolerance have repeatedly broken up communal peace and harmony. Reason has often lost its way in frenzied outpourings of religious zeal. Extremist religious ideologies as well as the violent politics of mindless forces on the right and the left have often overshadowed the idea of a tolerant society where many views would compete for public attention and where the motto 'live and let live' would be the nation's guiding philosophy.

This essay is a plea for the restoration of a liberal spirit in public life. It is written from the point of view of a liberal-secular democrat who also happens to be an agnostic. Some of the views I have expressed against organized religion in this book may offend some, for which I request forgiveness. I insist, however, that the right of a citizen to follow any faith is a fundamental, sacrosanct condition of life in secular India and that includes the right not to believe in a specific religion or to be an atheist.

The Partition of India in 1947 did not end debate in the republic called India over what exactly the personality of the nation should be. It may have settled the debate over national identity in the entity of Pakistan, though even that was, and perhaps remains, an open issue, with the violent breaking away of Bangladesh in 1971 highlighting the difficulty of defining a nation solely by religious identity. But, for India, the issue is not fully settled sixty years after the birth of the nation.

After the trauma of Partition, perhaps the single biggest controversy over the question of national identity to occupy our attention has been the Babri Masjid-Ram Janmabhoomi issue. When militants destroyed the mosque in December 1992, a fundamental debate ensued over what India should be. Which central idea forms the essence of any multiethnic, multi-religious nation? Must such a society uphold a particular culture that defines the core values of the nation? Or, must it not merely tolerate a wide variety of cultures but actually celebrate diversity?

Under the Allahabad High Court's ruling in October 2010, two-thirds of the disputed site in Ayodhya should go to Hindu groups, presumably for building a temple to Ram, while the remaining third should go to the Muslims for rebuilding the mosque. At the time of writing, we do not know whether the argument has ended with the court's decision. Perhaps it has, in a way. Violence, generally anticipated, did not break out following the verdict. But the court, by accepting the Hindu claim on the property, has implicitly acknowledged the Hindus' assertion that Ram, a mythological figure, had been born on that exact spot a few thousand years ago. The verdict was a typical instance of limp compromise that has marked India's experience and practice of secularism. This essay discusses India's peculiar and unsatisfactory interpretation of secularism.

I thank Yamini Lohia and Aditya Shajikumar for their invaluable assistance. I thank my wife, Rita Adhikari, for numerous suggestions on how to tackle the somewhat sensitive theme of this book. And I am grateful to Amit Agarwal for coming up with the idea of expanding a few thoughts that we had been discussing into a book. I also thank the Federation of Indian Chambers of Commerce and Industry and the East West Center in Washington DC for hosting me during part of my work on this essay.

Washington, DC GAUTAM ADHIKARI
9 January 2011

One

THE INTOLERANT INDIAN

It was the summer of 2002. On a pleasant evening in Washington DC, a conversation took place that should have alarmed me more than it initially did. At a festival of Satyajit Ray's movies organized by the Smithsonian Institution, my wife and I were chatting with friends near the entrance to the theatre where the evening's movie was about to be shown. A gentleman whom we knew well came up and asked in a sombre tone: 'Did you hear what happened in Gujarat today?' 'No,' I replied, not having browsed the Indian news websites that day.

'A bunch of bloody Muslims burnt a train carrying Hindu pilgrims at Godhra station,' he said, face hardening as he spoke. 'You know, Godhra, they say, has a 30 per cent Muslim population. Well, I think by tomorrow that percentage will be down to zero. And you secularist Indians can be free to lament your losses.'

As the man strolled off, I felt a little puzzled. I knew he leant towards a conservative view of life and, though not an activist himself, was known to have a pronounced sympathy for Hindu nationalist groups. However, chilling as his statement was, I didn't take it as an omen. Just shrugged it off as another one of those rants against Muslims I had heard from so many Indians living in the US. Little did I realize how close to accuracy that prediction would prove to be.

A hellfire consumed Gujarat over the next few days. As is well known and documented, Hindu fanatics went on the rampage while the police didn't seem to care very much. The state administration stood idly by as wild mobs stampeded through Muslim neighbourhoods, setting fire to homes, killing at random. Two thousand men, women and children, mostly Muslim, died in that spell of madness in the state. The rest of India was in shock, the national media screamed outrage, and the fanatics screamed back saying the Muslims got what they deserved. What continued to puzzle me was what the man had said that evening at the Ray film festival. I concluded he probably didn't know, from any source within the Sangh Parivar, that the carnage was about to happen. He was expressing his fury and wanted revenge. That in itself was not alarming, because we knew where he came from and had long agreed to disagree. What was disturbing was that in saying what he did he seemed to be echoing the feelings of millions, perhaps many millions, of intolerant Indians, some of whom would, over the next few days, make his macabre wish become real.

The intolerant Indian does not appreciate the idea of India. He sees India as a mirror image of what the founders of Pakistan saw as the idea of Pakistan, that is, a sanctuary for Muslims of the subcontinent who feared Hindu domination and a likely dilution of their Islamic identity in unified, secular India. The intolerant Indian believes that India should have been wrested back as a nation for Hindus not only from the Christian British but also from the Muslims, who had invaded and occupied this land for centuries and had just won a nation of their own through Partition. They should all, therefore, leave India, making this land pure for Hindus, just as the name Pakistan implies a land of the pure for Muslims. If some Muslims were to be left behind in India, they could be allowed to stay here so long as they sublimated their identity as Muslims to the broad identity of Hindu-ness or Hindutva.

This problem of identity as well as of the differing, sometimes violently clashing, ways in which we perceive India may be at the root of a fundamental dispute vexing the nation. It is between the intolerant Indian, who has an exclusivist, illiberal assumption of what the nation should be; and the liberal, who believes that the idea of India, as conceived by its founding fathers in recognition of the fault lines of history, is based on a tolerance of diversity, by nurturing which we can sustain a unified nation. The divisive debate fractures India.

The problem runs deep. The features that make so many of us proud of the variety of hues in our democratic canvas come from a liberal tradition that evolved in the world over a couple of centuries and influenced Indian nationalists who led the struggle for independence from British rule. At the same time, those are the very features that infuriate the intolerant traditionalist, who wants a singular Indian identity which, he believes, has emerged through the nationalist movement by the rediscovery of roots of an ancient, fundamentally Hindu, civilization.

The intolerant Indian assumes many faces. It would be erroneous to assume that the radical Hindu is the only incarnation of intolerance in India today. Intolerance thrives in the name of Islam, as I shall elaborate later in the book. Members of almost every major religious group, including Christians and Sikhs, have at some point or other fallen prey to instigators of intolerance. Indeed, it's not religious fanatics alone who spew venom; other apostles of hatred periodically burn scars in the fabric of India, from regional-linguistic exclusionists to caste or class combatants claiming victimhood.

It is, however, dangerous to play around with the idea of India. This is a unique experiment in democratic nation building, more complex than any other such attempt in human history. No nation exists, or has ever existed, which shelters under one flag anywhere near such a range of diversity of language, ethnicity and religion as India does under the canopy of a democratic republican constitution. It is an exceptional venture that has comfortably outlasted other ambitious attempts to create one nation out of many, such as the former Soviet Union and Yugoslavia.

In fact, liberal democracy is the bedrock on which the Indian experiment rests. The wise founding fathers, who had their differences over the idea of India, agreed while formulating India's Constitution that no dictator or monarch could hold such a nation together. The British, who ruled over the largest tract of subcontinental territory that any empire builder ever had in India, actually ran a successful franchise, somewhat like a McDonalds network, of revenue extraction based, over much of the area, on a nominal subjugation of maharajas, nawabs and landlords, and by educating an elite set of Indians to help run the business. That was how the East India Company preferred to maintain its hold over this vast area of diversity. Problems began to bubble over when the British converted the Company's franchise into a formal empire in the mid-nineteenth century.

Intellectual guiding lights of the nationalist movement, such as Mahatma Gandhi and Rabindranath Tagore, insisted well before the Constituent Assembly met after independence that 'unity in diversity' would have to be the cultural-political foundation of the Indian nation when it eventually came into being. India had to be a democratic republic, the founding fathers knew in their hearts when they set about drafting a constitution for the new nation. The sheer scale of diversity would need institutional outlets to release the steam that would inevitably build up as our myriad differences of culture, ethnicity, language, caste, religion and sub-national inclination jostled with one another in independent India.

India is 5,000 years old, goes a fairly common claim made by traditionalists. That may be so, but has such continuity alone made it a melting pot as a nation? Or is it a cultural and ethnic mosaic that needs political recognition of its diversity? These are competing views of what India is or should be. Those who say that India has lasted over fifty centuries tend to view the numerous problems of developing India, the nation, as mere clouds on a grand sky of unity – clouds that will vanish because India is time-tested as great and indivisible. India is not new, they assert. India is being reconstructed after centuries of pillage by outsiders, the last of whom left in 1947.

Fortunately, the framers of the Constitution of India went along with the competing view that India may be an ancient civilization but it is a new nation. Its ancient culture was a mix of many interlinked cultures that have coexisted over the centuries to evolve a composite identity that encompasses a wide diversity in language, religion and ethnicity. It is nonetheless a new nation state – a great experiment in democracy.

Sixty years ago, many Western sages, including Winston Churchill, gave India little chance of surviving as a nation. India has defied such dire predictions by merely existing. It has, however, done so by maintaining a democratic framework of government. It has survived not despite democracy, as some suggest, but because of it. An independent commission organizes regular elections to Parliament and state assemblies, while an assertive, if exasperatingly slow-moving judiciary protects fundamental rights. Freedom of expression is guaranteed under Article 19 of the Constitution and an independent press uses that freedom day in and day out.

I can venture to suggest that no previous attempt at creating a republican democracy began quite as boldly as India's. Undoubtedly, the founding fathers of the United States of

America launched a pioneering venture, and their effort, enshrined in a remarkable constitution, stands testimony to their brilliance. They did not, however, go quite as far – understandably, perhaps, given the stage of social and political evolution in the eighteenth century – as to offer all its adult citizens the right to vote. It took a lot of time, right up to the mid-twentieth century, and intense argument, often violent, for the US to ensure that right for every adult citizen. India's founding fathers, however, extended that right from the day the Constitution came into force, on 26 January 1950. All Indians above the age of twenty-one, regardless of gender, caste or class, were free to exercise that right in the first general election in 1952.

By extending the vote to everyone, the framers of the Constitution were merely being pragmatic. A tradition of pluralism had long existed in Indian culture. India's political elite, as well as its military, had developed a liberal commitment to democracy, which they had imbibed from the West through the British, and they did not lose that commitment after independence. The British had also left behind an enabling legal and administrative structure, much of which survived the exercise in creating a blueprint for the governance of the new nation.

Soon, given the sharp ethnic, religious, linguistic and other socio-economic diversities of this enormous country, citizens realized that it would be difficult for any single group to control the state for long. Contending groups rapidly began appreciating the usefulness of a democratic process that incorporated checks and balances as well as multiple veto powers to keep rivals working as partners in coalitions. Even the early Congress party was a coalition of interests and of class, caste and regional groupings. However, the decline of the Congress system and the rise of coalition governments from 1989 was an inevitable result of the reality of India's national tapestry. It reflected the mosaic of India better than any melting pot assumption. Given that reality, perhaps no singular melting pot ideology can ever succeed here.

Far too often, however, that constitutionally defined image of a tolerant, liberal India – an India that understands and practises the maxim 'live and let live' – has been attacked by dissenters around the country. Governments, state as well as national, have capitulated more often than not to please one vote bank or the other, thus inflating a mere nuisance into a threat to our collective vision of India. But if those embers of exclusionary or sub-nationalistic zeal are not doused early, any resulting fire can cremate the current constitutionally defined idea of India, which to my mind is the only viable option we have to sustain this remarkable venture.

Democracy is a grand principle to which we are all constitutionally committed. Even so, many of us do not seem to appreciate a foundational feature of a liberal democratic society: that it is as much about majority rule as about making minorities – religious, ethnic, racial or just different in thought or practice from the dominant cultural norm – feel not only safe but comfortable enough to freely pursue their life goals.

The problem goes to the heart of how we view India. The features that make us proud of the dazzling variety in our democratic canvas can only coexist with one another within a liberal tradition that has evolved in the world over the past couple of centuries. Ideas born out of that tolerant tradition do not fit in with primordial feelings of exclusivity or with any rigid notion of the 'other' in society.

Tolerance of differences on a nationwide scale requires a high degree of personal liberty to be guaranteed by the constitution of any liberal democratic state. The Constitution of India reflects recognition of India's diversity by spelling out a series of fundamental rights that add up to a classically liberal view of the world. It guarantees those judicially enforceable civil and political rights in broad categories such as equality before the law, freedom of expression, assembly and association, freedom of movement within India, and the freedom to carry on a profession, trade, or business. Freedom of conscience and the right to profess, practise and propagate religion is guaranteed. Minorities have the right to conserve a language, script or culture and to run educational institutions. Under Article 21, no person can be deprived of life or personal liberty except according to procedure established by law. Still, there are problems with the way some provisions have been written or amended into the Indian Constitution, as we shall see.

Fundamental rights in the Constitution are real and legally enforceable. As no right can be absolute, the exercise of a fundamental right can be reasonably restricted by law enacted in the public interest. In exercise of their power of judicial review, courts in India have struck down laws which in their view imposed restrictions that were either arbitrary or excessive. The courts have also often stepped in to protect the liberty of citizens in a series of celebrated cases.

For instance, the clause guaranteeing freedom of expression does not specify freedom of the press, as the first amendment to the American constitution does. Therefore, in a number of decisions, the Supreme Court of India ruled that freedom of the press was implicit in the guarantee of freedom of expression. In a case involving Bennett, Coleman & Co, the holding company of *The Times of India* group, the Supreme Court described freedom of the press as 'the Ark of the Covenant of Democracy'. State high courts too have similarly ruled in a number of cases, underlining the view that freedom of the press is a fundamental right.

The courts in India have gone to great lengths to uphold the constitutional guarantee of freedom of expression. In one case, the Supreme Court even ruled that the guarantee included the right not to speak, when three Jehovah's Witnesses complained that they had had been expelled from an educational institution for having refused to sing the national anthem because their religion forbade them from singing the anthem of any country. They had stood up when the anthem was being sung but had remained silent. The court ruled in favour of the three, declaring that the expulsion violated their right to freedom of expression. Thus, in one stroke, the court upheld the right to free speech as well as the right to profess and practise a religion.

Even though excruciatingly tardy in delivering judgments, the courts have time and again stepped in to protect personal liberty guaranteed by the fundamental rights listed in the Constitution. It is another matter that the implementation of judgments by the executive often falls woefully short of the requirement. Thus, the Supreme Court has ruled, in a case involving numerous individuals held without trial in prisons in Bihar, that no one could be deprived of personal liberty except under a procedure established by law. These undertrials, as they are euphemistically called, had been imprisoned for periods longer than the maximum period of the sentence they would have received had they been convicted by a court. The court said that any procedure that allowed detention of undertrials for periods longer than the maximum sentence permitted upon conviction was a violation of the fundamental right to life and liberty spelt out in Article 21. The prisoners, therefore, had to be released. Even so, to this day thousands of Indians continue to languish in prison without trial in clear violation of Article 21.

Tardy implementation by the executive of constitutional provisions or court judgments, however, is not the only problem hampering the effective translation of the liberal character of the Constitution into living practice. There are two other impediments. A major one is the poor and, in my view, declining comprehension and acceptance, since independence, of tolerant liberalism by the people at large as well as by most leading political groups and ideological camps. I shall discuss the issue at some length later as it forms the central concern of this essay.

The other, relatively minor, hitch lies in the Constitution itself, specifically in some compromising qualifications that accompany several of the clauses spelling out fundamental rights. Take the protection of the right to freedom of speech. Article 19(a) states that all citizens have 'the right to freedom of speech and expression', but this clear statement is quickly followed by Article 19(2), which says that nothing in that sub-clause shall affect the operation of any law, or prevent the state from making any law to impose 'reasonable restrictions' on the exercise of that right in the interest of 'the sovereignty and integrity of India, the security of the State, friendly relations with foreign States, public order, decency or morality or in relation to contempt of court, defamation or incitement to an offence'.

In short, that fundamental right remains a right unless the government thinks otherwise in the name of a range of concerns that cover a gamut of public policies. This is very different, for instance, from the provision of freedom of speech in the US Constitution, in which the first amendment states categorically: 'Congress shall make no law respecting an establishment of religion or prohibiting the free exercise thereof, or abridging the freedom of speech, or of the press, or the right of people peaceably to assemble, and to petition the government for a redress of grievances.'

Therefore, what might constitute 'reasonable restrictions' to be imposed by a government on the exercise of free speech is a matter that the courts in India have had to periodically determine. It must also be said that, with the exception of the nineteen-month period of a state of Emergency imposed by Prime Minister Indira Gandhi during 1975-77, no government has, by and large, tried to censor or legally curtail the right of people, and of the press, to express their views and opinions, though censorship of films remains a grey area where the government formally intervenes.

Perhaps the framers of India's Constitution, while adding

sub-clause (2) to Article 19(a), had borne in mind, first, the needs of a fledgling democracy and a nation-in-the-making and, second, the experience of America, where freedom of speech, and of the press, undoubtedly flowed but also periodically ebbed through the late eighteenth and nineteenth centuries. It was not until the twentieth century, following a number of court judgments accompanied by a rising tide of liberal politics, that the right to freedom of expression was firmly, and admirably, established in the US. Nevertheless, in India's case, the ambiguity embedded in that sub-clause of Article 19 remains open to misinterpretation, and possible misuse, given a weakening appreciation of liberal values at the political and popular levels of public opinion.

Such ambiguities exist in the way some other key features of the Constitution were drafted or, in some instances, amended. For example, Article 15 prohibits discrimination 'on grounds of religion, race, caste, sex or place of birth', but sub-clause 4 says that this article cannot prevent the state 'from making any special provision for the advancement of any socially and educationally backward classes of citizens or for the Scheduled Castes and the Schedule Tribes'. Article 16, which promises equality of opportunity in public employment, is no different in essence and its sub-clauses make similar exceptions for the government to discriminate in certain cases. The Constitution therefore permits positive discrimination in the form of affirmative action by the government on behalf of certain castes and tribes, which is perhaps as it should be, for these groups have a history of negative discrimination against them over centuries. The problem, as it transpired, is that many more castes and groups began to claim and obtain the special provisions allowed by the sub-clauses in Article 15 and 16, thereby transforming affirmative action, initially granted for a period of ten years, into a reserved quota system covering a large number of castes and sub-castes who saw themselves as exploited. In consequence, the jobs reservation system spun out of control. A reasonable and supposedly temporary policy of helping the most deprived castes and tribes became a growing and permanent quota-based facility.

Ambiguities in how the Indian Constitution spells out fundamental rights are, however, to my mind, less problematic than certain words inserted in the preamble of the document. These were inserted not in 1949, when the preamble was initially written, but in 1976, when constitutional liberty had been temporarily suspended.

A constitution outlines the vision that a nation's people have, or ought to have, of themselves in their aspiration to live in a sovereign country. A preamble sets out the context in which the provisions that follow can be better understood. In India's case, the Supreme Court ruled in 1973 that the preamble contained the 'basic structure' of our Constitution. The preamble, as it now reads, thus states the nation's goals:

> We, the people of India, having solemnly resolved to constitute India into a sovereign socialist secular democratic republic and to secure to all its citizens:
> Justice, social, economic and political;
> Liberty of thought, expression, belief, faith and worship;
> Equality of status and opportunity; and to promote among them all

> Fraternity assuring the dignity of the individual and the unity and integrity of the Nation...

That was not how it read when the founding fathers signed the document in November 1949. The words 'socialist' and 'secular' came in when Indira Gandhi, during her Emergency rule (1975-77), pushed the forty-second amendment of the Constitution through a docile Parliament. So did the bit about the 'unity and integrity' of the nation. The words, taken together, perhaps achieved a political need at the time – on the advice of CPI leftists, Indira Gandhi wanted to appear as socialist as possible, besides wanting to secure Muslim support by making the Constitution formally secular. However, the amendment introduced in the preamble a confusion that persists to this day in our vision of the nation's goals.

The words 'sovereign' and 'democratic' were and remain fairly clear. They are easy to define with reasonable precision. Not so 'socialist' and not, as it turned out in the Indian context, the term 'secular'. Also, whereas 'unity' of the nation is more or less easily understood, what does the preamble mean by 'integrity' of the nation?

For the purpose of this discussion, the reference to the unity and integrity of the nation is not a problem area. More relevant to our concern about illiberal tendencies and intolerance are the words 'socialist' and 'secular'. Did the insertion of 'socialist' alter the fundamentally liberal democratic character of the republic as envisioned in the original Constitution? Also, despite the assertion of the preamble after the forty-second amendment, is the Indian state really secular in the conventionally accepted sense of the term or is Indian secularism an amorphous concept that we can only treat as a special case?

Nowhere in the original Constitution will you find any statement or assertion that India was to be a socialist nation. Not even Jawaharlal Nehru, with his pronounced sympathy for the socialist cause, preached socialism as the national ideology, though he did speak of a 'socialistic pattern of society' and of a 'mixed economy'. Article 19(1)(f) of the original text actually gave the individual a fundamental right to own private property; this provision was specifically removed in 1978, when the then Janata government inserted the forty-fourth amendment to the Constitution, thus tilting the nation further in the direction of state control and state ownership of production and business. The Constitution still allows an individual the right to run a business, and permits the ownership of private property, but after the forty-fourth amendment, no court in India can disallow confiscatory legislation or declare any such state action as violating the provisions of the Constitution.

Therefore, although India, in its economic and social aspirations, seems to be moving away from socialism and an ambitious middle class is rising with ideas of its own on how to run the country, the state retains the right to be socialist if it so chooses. That indeed is only the legal position. Ideologically, much of the Indian political spectrum comes in socialist hues. Socialist, and even communist, ideas as well as rhetoric continue to command considerable sway over public debate, notwithstanding the global demise of socialism and communism as fountainheads of ideological inspiration.

In reality, India has never been socialist. It has from its early days as an independent republic been at best an attempt at social democracy, albeit one with a fluctuating dose, during its first forty years or so, of heavy-handed state control of production and business. Since the beginning of a process of economic liberalization in 1991, economic thinking in India has steadily moved away from socialistic ideas. However, in political ideology, the country has failed to create any meaningful or even noticeable space for what socialists and Marxists contemptuously call 'bourgeois liberalism'. Yet that bourgeois liberalism is precisely what has always been a founding principle of modern democracy. It never existed in the Soviet Union and does not exist in today's China, which has an economy running on broad market principles but tightly controlled by the Communist Party. The Chinese are not liberal in any sense of the term and have to qualify their claim to democracy as a 'people's democracy'. Also, fundamental rights for the individual do not form a part of the Chinese system of justice and fair play as they do crucially in a society based on genuine liberalism.

That liberalism, into which are seamlessly woven the ideas of tolerance and individual liberty, rests on principles which formed an early vision of what the Indian republic should be. Such liberal thinking permeates the Indian Constitution in its original form. Its essence is as far away from socialism and communism as it is from hatred, and religious and caste-based identity politics. I shall examine this issue later.

The insertion of the word 'secular' in the preamble was quite redundant. The idea of India was secular in character to begin with because it was not Pakistan. Pakistan was created specifically for those Muslims of the subcontinent who felt they could not continue to live in 'Hindu-dominated' India. India was, therefore, secular for the rest of us, including those Muslims who did not want to leave their homes for Pakistan. In that sense, India was the non-Pakistan; a sanctuary of religious tolerance in which people professing different faiths would live in harmony and the state would be formally secular. A majority of leaders of independent India, under the leadership of Jawaharlal Nehru, agreed, notwithstanding the strong reservations of some, that they had to create a secular state if the new nation was to sustain itself in unity as a democratic republic amidst a plethora of religious diversity.

Indeed, the freedom movement, under Mahatma Gandhi's guidance, had long recognized the importance of secularism in a nation housing so many faiths. Even when the dreams of an undivided India lay broken in the trauma of Partition, the founding fathers of India remained steadfast in their adherence to secularism. That was why they wrote Articles 25 to 31 into the Constitution, giving everyone the entitlement to freely practise religion. That fundamental right is literally for everyone, including foreigners residing here, and not just for citizens of India. Article 25 says, 'All persons are equally entitled to freedom of conscience and the right freely to profess, practise and propagate religion.' In short, though secularism was not expressly mentioned in the preamble to the Constitution, it was very intrinsic to the spirit of the document.

As mentioned earlier, the insertion of the word in the preamble in 1976 was a political move by Indira Gandhi's government, which sought to secure the long-term loyalty of minorities by dramatically demonstrating its credentials for pluralist tolerance. It was also aimed against non-secular political ideologies, such as the Jana Sangh's in those days, to score yet another political point. In 1978, the Janata government, which had been voted to power a year before when the state of Emergency had been lifted, tried to introduce an amendment explaining a 'secular republic' to mean 'a republic in which there is equal respect for all religions', but the Congress, which still commanded a majority in the upper house of Parliament, rejected it.

What exactly being 'secular' means in the Indian context, however, remains somewhat vague. It is clearly not a strict separation of church and state, as it is understood to mean in several European nations and the US. Indian secularism implies equal respect for all religions, the liberty of belief, faith, and worship, and a pluralist tolerance of religious differences by the state as well as by citizens. However, whether the state should stay out of religious affairs altogether and whether religious authorities in turn must stay out of the affairs of state is not specified in the Indian Constitution, even after the insertion of the word 'secular' in the preamble.

Therefore, secularism in India is a more flexible concept than it should perhaps be, as I shall discuss later.

Be that as it may, for an Indian being secular clearly means being tolerant. That indeed is what I had wanted to tell my acquaintance at the Ray film festival that evening in 2002, when he had said that he wanted a massacre of Muslims to avenge what a bunch of Muslims had allegedly done in burning a train and killing Hindus at Godhra railway station that day. Yes, I had wanted to say, if some Muslim hooligans had endulged in such an act, the police should round them up and punish them under the law after trial and conviction, not for being Muslim but for being violent arsonists. What he had wanted, for his part, was vengeance on all Muslims in Godhra, not for being criminals, which most of them clearly weren't, but for being Muslims.

Two

PLURALISM AND TOLERANCE

A few days after the results had been announced in Gujarat's state elections of late 2007, Ashis Nandy, a social psychologist, contributed an op-ed article to *The Times of India*. As I was looking after the opinions section of the newspaper, I took a close look at one paragraph which seemed to chastise the entire Gujarati middle class for being irresponsible in re-electing the Bharatiya Janata Party, once again with Narendra Modi as chief minister of the state. My colleagues and I decided to let it pass, as we felt it was the personal view of the writer, a public intellectual, writing for a page of the newspaper reserved for a range of opinions which were not all necessarily identical to ours. We carried the article on our editorial page on 8 January 2008.

By the next morning, and for a few weeks afterwards, email messages from angry supporters of Hindutva and

Modi flooded my mailbox. Although written in the kind of language we wouldn't normally allow on the pages of a family newspaper, several were sufficiently imaginative to generate a smile. One curious emailer questioned my Indian ancestry; he said my late mother had actually been a Pakistani Muslim. Another thought I had been born in Afghanistan into a Taliban family. Several compared me to a variety of animals, especially the dog and the pig, and one called *The Times of India* a menagerie of Hindu-haters. Ashis Nandy phoned in to say he had received similarly affectionate messages and had consulted a lawyer in the event of anyone in Gujarat taking him to court. There was, however, one email that I found particularly fascinating for both its painstaking construction and its colourful vitriol.

It was a power-point presentation which had apparently been circulated widely. It lampooned *The Times of India*, ridiculed our journalists, and in the final panel, described us as a 'banana newspaper', whatever that might mean. It, however, gave me an opportunity to explain what a liberal newspaper, banana or not, was all about.

The central point in need of clarification was that Nandy's article was published on the basis of the quality of his writing and the logical consistency of what he had to say. It reflected his view and that was why the article had been carried under his name. It did not necessarily coincide, thought for thought, with the newspaper's editorial position on the Gujarat election results. These we had elaborately set out for readers a few days earlier in the unsigned column reserved for expressing the paper's views, though there were several points on which our views coincided with Nandy's.

In a column I wrote a few days after Nandy's article had been published and the barrage of hate mail had begun, I tried to explain how a daily newspaper's opinion section worked and pointed out that the distinguishing mark of a liberal newspaper, as opposed to a hardline or ideologically extremist one, was the plurality of signed views of columnists and other contributors it would carry as opinion pieces. Thus, we had carried a number of columns highly favourable to Modi and the BJP, just as we had made space for critical columns like Nandy's. True, our own bias towards liberalism and tolerance would influence our choice; but we would consciously attempt to carry as many reasonably presented diverse viewpoints as we could.

Explanations of that kind, however, never appeal to extremists who are not looking for logic outside their closed systems of thought. The email barrage continued for several days, until perhaps the senders became bored of their target and moved on.

It is not, however, the extremists alone who should concern us. Liberalism, tolerance and acceptance of diversity do not seem to come that easily to many of India's politicians and intellectuals, even though the Constitution was founded on liberal principles. Strange as it may sound for a nation conceived by such savants as Gandhi, Tagore and Nehru, it is actually difficult to find a truly liberal space on India's political spectrum. None of the political parties in India can really be constitutionally 'liberal', that is, support an open economy and believe in individual autonomy, for under the Constitution as it stands now, all parties have to believe in socialism.

There is a fiercely Hindu nationalist segment, led by the RSS and the BJP on the right of the political spectrum; a bunch of dogmatic and outdated Marxist parties and intellectuals on the left; while the Congress, a few casteist and regionally affiliated parties, and some waffling socialists form a muddle in the middle. The Congress speaks tolerance but its record on the ground leaves a trail of confused thinking at best, and cynical manoeuvring at worst, particularly during the Emergency.

In fact, any political party professing a market-oriented economy within a classically liberal framework could be ruled out of action for being unconstitutional. As we have seen in the first chapter, the preamble to the Indian Constitution requires the nation to be 'socialist' and there is no fundamental right to private property. Classical liberalism, or for that matter even post-Keynesian liberalism (which, unlike classical liberalism, provides for welfare or even deficit spending), requires the right to private property and the freedom to choose offered by a market-oriented system. There can be differences among liberals – the very definition demands the airing of differences – about the role of the state and how far it should go to regulate profiteering or to curb monopolies or to monitor banking or to ensure equitable tax structures. In India, however, as the law stands today, a political party must first accept socialism as an economic-ideological doctrine before being able to operate legally.

Of course, what is meant by socialism has not been defined in the Constitution. Is it a full-blown form of socialism, providing full state control over the economy and with no right to private property? Is it Gandhian socialism, which is a different idea altogether with its decentralized village economies and a scaling back of rapid urbanizing growth as we commonly understand it? Or is it a bit of this and a bit of that, adding up to nothing more than a rhetorical device to help politicians sound egalitarian? In fact, it amounts to no more than a phony word in today's India, which is liberalizing its economy and encouraging the growth of business as well as foreign private investment.

At the same time, even as the Constitution preaches tolerance, the state caves in to sectarian and extremist demands, such as when orthodox Muslims attack Bangladeshi writer Taslima Nasrin and demand that she must not be sheltered in India; or when bigoted Hindus attack exhibitions showing M. F. Husain's works because he has drawn Saraswati or other Hindu goddesses in a semi-nude form. Rather than standing firm and insisting that everyone has a right to free expression, governments, both state and Central, ban books in pursuit of vote banks.

The nation was born in blood. As the inevitability of Partition became increasingly obvious, tensions heightened between Hindus and Muslims, especially in those states which were likely to be partitioned. Without going into the history of how that tension came about or how the idea of Partition gained ground in the 1940s, we can note that the long spell of communal riots of 1946-47 was the bloodiest in the subcontinent's history, and the scars of that carnage continue to haunt India.

In pursuit of its demand for a separate state of Pakistan, the Muslim League in still undivided India set the ball rolling. It designated 16 August 1946 as Direct Action Day in Calcutta in the hope of polarizing the two communities to a point where the British would have no option but to leave behind two separate nations when they finally left. 'Direct action' was technically a call for strikes, rallies and public meetings; in the highly charged political atmosphere of Calcutta at that time, it was an all but open call to violence. Riots broke out in the city and lasted nearly a week. Then they spread to Noakhali in East Bengal and to Bihar, where thousands died.

Although Muslims had ignited the fuse in Calcutta, they were a minority in that city.They were consequently the principal victims of the riots. In Noakhali, Hindus were the principal victims; in Bihar, it was the Muslims again who bore the brunt of the massacre.

Rioting did not consume the rest of the country at that juncture. Some violence occurred in Bombay and Uttar Pradesh but Punjab was still quiet. Not for long, though. As the day of independence approached and the boundaries of the two countries were to be announced by the British, the killings began to spread through Punjab. Its Muslim majority fiercely wanted Pakistan; its Hindu and Sikh minorities became increasingly fearful that their homeland would be divided. Rioting took place in Punjab, killing thousands, throughout the first half of 1947. It wasn't, however, until Partition actually happened that mere rioting turned into mass slaughter in Punjab and Delhi. Possibly, over a million died.

Thus, the nation was born in a storm of intolerance. An immediate cause must have been the hurt that people felt on being forced to leave home for what appeared to be no fault of theirs. But a deeper cause was probably a smouldering resentment of the 'other' born out of deliberate fanning of identity politics and religious nationalism.

Historians and sociologists have written volumes in their effort to understand the roots of that resentment – particularly in the context of Hindu-Muslim relations – and have come up with a range of explanations. Conservative Hindus see the relationship as primordially antagonistic, with a superior and ancient Hindu nation being attacked and oppressed for centuries by a group of foreign invaders who sought to impose their Islamic values and belief system on India but failed. At the other extreme are radical Islamists who seek to deny that there was any oppression of Hindus at all by Muslim rulers, dubbing it a myth created by Hindu ideologues.

In all probability, the reality conforms to neither of the extremes. Not just two tightly bound or clearly identifiable communities, but several must have existed in pre-British India, or as many as the caste system would have allowed. There was, however, a dominant ruling elite in a large part of India which was Muslim and clearly self-identified as a community, and there were pockets dominated by caste-Hindu elites. The general masses, comprising a broad range of castes, later became known as Hindus as well as non-elite, converted Muslims. There were also other communities, including tribal groups, Sikhs, Christians and a number of low-caste untouchables.

From available accounts, it does not appear that there was intermarriage, inter-dining, or significant intermingling among these communities on the social plane, though many of them, barring the Muslims and Christians, had not yet self-identified themselves as belonging to any particular religious community to distinguish themselves from other similarly self-identified groups. That happened later, in the nineteenth century, partly as a direct result of colonial influence, and partly in reaction to colonial rule and on the back of a growing nationalist movement.

To cite an instance of the colonial impact, take the first-ever census exercise in the subcontinent, which began in 1872. After suppressing the uprising of 1857 in northern India, the British formally moved to make their Indian acquisition an empire, and Queen Victoria became Empress of India in 1860. A group of officials soon began a census exercise in order to enumerate and classify the population, estimated at that time to be around 250 million, perhaps with an eye to exercising better control over their subjects. The exercise hierarchically classified castes and divided the population into different religious communities, of which the two major ones were 'Hindu' and 'Muslim'. The Hindus were classified as the 'majority' and the Muslims as a 'minority', thus laying out a future pathway to representative politics.

There are two schools of thought as to why the British went in for such a classification of separate communities. Some historians and nationalists believe that it was a devious colonial plot to 'divide and rule'. Others believe it was a part of the modernizing enterprise of colonial rule, aimed at increasing understanding as well as efficiency, but that it created divisions that were exploited by subsequent British rulers to their advantage, and that led eventually to

Partition of the subcontinent. To suggest, however, that no tension or antagonistic relations whatsoever existed between communities in pre-colonial days would obviously be incorrect.

The process of documentation of data of various kinds initiated by the colonial rulers undoubtedly created a body of knowledge about India. It led to the census and also to the creation of dictionaries and grammars of Indian languages as well as codification of Hindu and Muslim laws. In turn, the exercise might have strengthened a process of consolidating communal, as well as linguistic, ethnic and racial identities.

However, separate communities existed and contested one another in pre-colonial India. For instance, during the reigns of some Mughal emperors, particularly Aurangzeb, temples were destroyed and mosques built over such sites in state-sponsored operations. The imposition of taxes on non-Muslims was also an intermittent feature of Muslim rule. History also records examples of Hindu kings creating and imposing on their subjects a society based on the ideology of Hinduism, such as in Jaipur in the eighteenth century.

Differences also existed within the broader categories of communities. Apart from the numerous caste differences within the Hindu community, there was a sharp distinction between caste Hindus and untouchables in pre-colonial India. This, of course, persists to this day, causing much political and social bitterness, despite legislation outlawing such distinctions. There were perceived differences of race, which also remain prevalent within communities. Fair-skinned Muslim elites, for example, proudly tended to consider their origin as foreign to the Indian soil and liked to distinguish themselves from low-caste converts of native roots. Although treating Muslims as 'foreign' to India, and conversely seeing Hindus as sons of the soil, may be a narrative created in colonial times within a section of nationalists, the feeling persists among elite Muslims too as a measure of class distinction.

Sometimes, this attitude of being 'foreign', and consequently superior, generates amusing assumptions among subcontinental Muslims, as I witnessed once. At a dinner party in a Bangladeshi friend's house, my wife and I happened to be the only non-Bangladeshi invitees but the other guests were unaware of our nationality. We listened as a robust conversation began on art and architecture in the subcontinent. Many asserted that India wrongly claimed Islamic art for itself and had brazenly usurped great landmarks of Mughal architecture, such as the Taj Mahal, as Indian.

'After all, we brought that architecture and art from Persia and now the Hindus say it's theirs,' said one woman. 'The Taj is ours.' Most of the others nodded in agreement. Apart from our host, that is, who gently intervened, 'Pardon me, but who is this "we" you are referring to? As far as I am aware, the ancestors of most of us in this room were local peasants and fishermen who converted to Islam. We are not Persians, are we?'

What kind of a nation should India be? That it should be a democratic republic was not much in dispute when the

Constituent Assembly deliberated the matter. The question of whether it should be a secular state or be a nation primarily for the majority community, that is, Hindus, was a more contentious issue. The founding fathers eventually settled on an idea of India which assumed within it a notion of who we are, but the question was not fully resolved. Secular nationalists, led by Nehru, won the argument, as we shall see, but not everyone agreed with their view.

The Partition of the subcontinent had not resolved the question of national identity of the part that was to be the Republic of India. The Muslim-majority areas of Bengal and Punjab had become Pakistan, but India retained a huge Muslim minority. There were thirty million Muslims scattered across the country and they were fearful for their future. They had to be integrated in the new republic, along with other minorities.

The leadership of the Congress party, which had led the struggle for independence and found itself after Partition in charge of defining an identity for the nation, thought it essential for India's nationhood to be rooted in secular principles. The people living in the new nation would be bound by citizenship in a democracy where religious identity would not be a hurdle to full participation in political, social and economic activity. The Indian nation should be inclusive, plural and tolerant.

Not everyone agreed. There were Hindus who rejected the pluralist vision of free India, which was the India of Nehru and Gandhi. The Hindu Mahasabha and the Rashtriya Swayamsevak Sangh, or RSS, thought India should be Hindustan, the land of the Hindus, especially as Pakistan, a land for Muslims, had been carved out of what they saw as a holy land.

The Hindu Mahasabha, which was the most important Hindu organization in India prior to independence, saw Indian nationhood in unambiguously religious terms. Its leader, V.D. Savarkar, wrote in his 1925 treatise *Hindutva:* 'A Hindu means a person who regards this land of Bharat Varsha, from the Indus to the seas, as his fatherland as well as his holy land that is the cradle of his religion.' In his view, an Indian was a Hindu, period. All other religious communities must defer to the wishes of the majority community, which should rightfully rule India as a Hindu state.

From its early stages in the nineteenth century, Indian nationalism had been tinged with flavours of religious nationalism. This was true for Hindus as well as for Muslims and Sikhs. In the early twentieth century, an inclusive, religion-neutral, secular nationalism became the guiding principle of the independence movement, until the demand of the Muslim League for a separate land for Muslims once again revived religious nationalism and led to a bloody partition of the country. In that sense, Savarkar's equating Hindutva with Indian nationhood was rooted in the ideas of an Indian nation in the nineteenth and early twentieth centuries. Secularism was a new concept and harder to sell.

The RSS was founded in 1925 in Maharashtra by K.B. Hedgewar. He drew inspiration from the Maratha warrior-leader Shivaji, who challenged the Mughal Empire and whose successors took the fight to the British. Consequently, the RSS initially had a strong Maharashtrian base; but its influence gradually spread throughout the Hindi-speaking region of north and central India. It is today the ideological as well as organizational backbone of the Hindu nationalist movement known as the Sangh Parivar, and is represented in politics and Parliament by the BJP. It is formally not a religious body – it merely believes in a healthy body and a healthy mind for individuals to create a strong nation – nor is it a political party. However, as we shall see, though it emphasizes discipline and spiritualism, and not any specific religious ritual or custom, its version of nationalism is based on a radical interpretation of Hinduism that claims tolerance as a guiding principle but is, in reality, highly exclusionary.

It was not just the nationalist movement, however, that had a significant element of religious identity; some reform movements of Hinduism in the nineteenth and early twentieth centuries, while espousing tolerance, held within them seeds of an exclusivist tendency.

Both the Arya Samaj, founded by Dayanand Saraswati, and the Ramakrishna Mission, started by Vivekananda, rose from a desire of some progressive Hindus, who were uneasy at the prospect of a European-influenced Westernizing and Christianizing tendency arising in the country, to resist orthodoxy and reform the religion. As both the movements arose through Hinduism's encounter with European thought and the Christian religion, each had certain elements borrowed from the foreign tradition, as indeed was the idea of nationalism itself. Dayanand wanted Hindusim to be a religion of the Book, which it wasn't in any sense as Christianity was, and wanted Hindus to return to their Vedic roots. Vivekananda, while denouncing Western materialism and stressing the superiority of Hindu spiritualism, modelled his new ascetic and discipline-based order of monks, the Ramakrishna Mission, on the Society of Jesus. The ideas of both these reformers influenced the ideas of religious nationalists as well as of Mahatma Gandhi.

Dayanand asserted that the Hindu nation had fallen on hard times because Hindus had moved away from Vedic fundamentals. He wanted to re-establish the authority of the Vedas. He exhorted his followers not to worship images and to abolish the divisions of caste, which had crippled Hindu capacities. Yet, apparently in the interest of organizing Hindus along nationalist lines, the Arya Samajists joined the orthodoxy in calling for a cow protection movement to defend Hinduism against the 'butchery' of Muslims and Christians. The Arya Samaj's spread remained restricted to north-western India, but its ideas exerted some influence on Hindu nationalists.

Vivekananda, who had educated himself extensively in Western thought, sought to integrate the many strands of Hindu tradition into a coherent notion of spirituality, which he asserted was superior to the materialism that had been introduced to India by the imperial British. His spiritualism and tolerant-inclusive version of Hinduism influenced Gandhi, as did his exhortations to uplift the poor and lower castes. His emphasis on ascetic discipline, resulting in healthy minds and bodies, influenced the Hindu nationalists. His aim was to link nationalism with spiritualism and social reform to revive a weakened Hindu nation.

It is relevant to point out here that the popularly accepted notion of an inclusive and tolerant Hindu culture, which nationalist ideologies imbibed, was and remains a debatable assumption. In the view of some scholars, the universal idea of 'tolerance' and Hindu 'inclusiveness' are not coterminous. Whereas tolerance must necessarily be all-inclusive, the Hindu nationalist version of inclusive tolerance implies a hierarchy of acceptance. Muslims or untouchables are low in the hierarchical order and their acceptance in the Hindu concept of inclusiveness is correspondingly as outsiders. In the case of Muslims, or Christians for that matter, their refusal to be part of any Hindu nationalist consensus automatically disqualifies them from tolerance. In other words, their very intolerance in not agreeing to be part of the Vedantic tradition, places them outside the pale of Hindu tolerance, which is otherwise alive and open for numerous competing Hindu-Indian groups. Pluralist tolerance in the Hindu nationalist view is a qualified concept.

If Hindu nationalists thought India should be a land for Hindus just as Pakistan would be a land for Muslims, the majority of India's other nationalists felt, by and large, that India should be a secular nation in which every citizen would be free to exercise full constitutional rights and there would be no discrimination on the basis of religion. However, the secularism they promoted was not a strict separation of church and state. Secularism in India became a different concept and whether it should still be termed as such is a question that is not easy to answer.

At the time of independence and through the early years of the republic, leaders of the Congress party, which had led the nationalist movement and had assumed the responsibility for governing the country, were not unanimous on how secular India should be. Nehru, the Westernized liberal, had a certain view, Vallabhbhai Patel another. Nehru's view eventually prevailed but it did not happen without challenge.

Nehru was partial to universal ideas, led a Western lifestyle, and remained a liberal to his last breath, even though his love of liberalism was tinged with an equal fondness for socialism. Patel, Nehru's deputy in the new government, had many supporters in the Congress leadership ranks. He was a home-grown nationalist, a teetotaller, and an austere, disciplined man. They had different views on how to treat minorities in the new India, and on this issue Patel had more supporters in the party than did Nehru.

In Patel's view, minorities in India would have to assume the responsibility of proving their loyalty to the majority community. Muslims, in particular, should 'remove doubts and misgivings entertained by a large section of the people about their loyalty founded largely on their past association with the demand for Pakistan and the unfortunate activities of some of them.' Nehru, on the other hand, thought it was the responsibility of the Congress and the government to make Muslims feel secure in India; to ensure that security, India would have to be tolerant, plural and secular.

As social scientist Ramachandra Guha has noted, the first president of the Indian state, Rajendra Prasad, was close to Patel. So was Purshottamdas Tandon, who was elected president of the Congress party in August 1950, much to Nehru's chagrin.

Following Tandon's election as party president, Nehru

was sufficiently distressed to issue a statement to the press saying that the 'spirit of communalism and revivalism has gradually invaded the Congress'. That 'communalist and reactionary forces' had openly rejoiced at Tandon's victory upset him deeply. As India, unlike Pakistan, was a secular state, minorities would have to be treated in exactly the same way as the majority. 'Indeed, fair treatment is not enough; we have to make them feel they are so treated,' declared Nehru.

The prime minister also had sharp differences with the president of India on the question of secularism. When he received an invitation to inaugurate a newly restored Somnath temple in Gujarat, Rajendra Prasad decided to accept it against Nehru's advice asking him not to participate in the reopening of a temple that had been the subject of historical discord between Hindus and Muslims. The Somnath temple had been raided through the centuries by several Muslim marauders, starting with Mahmud of Ghazni in the eleventh century. Hindus had rebuilt the temple each time it had been destroyed until the Mughal emperor Aurangzeb had ordered its total destruction. Rebuilt again after two-and-a-half centuries of lying in ruins, the temple was a standing symbol of communal tension.

In Nehru's view, public officials in a secular state should never associate publicly with religious functions or officially participate in celebrations of events at shrines. Rajendra Prasad, however, felt that visiting the Somnath shrine was fine because, as he said in a speech at the inauguration of the temple, he believed in tolerance of all religions. 'I respect all religions and on occasion visit a church, a dargah and a gurdwara,' he said, although he remained a Hindu by faith. So it was that at the very outset of the Indian national enterprise, there emerged two competing views of secular public behaviour, which have never been altogether reconciled to this day.

What kind of secular state did Nehru have in mind? Although India was undoubtedly a deeply religious country, it was not as if affairs of the state could not be kept separate from religion. However, Indian leaders, including Nehru, opted for a Gandhian interpretation of secularism, which implied tolerance of all religions but did not require the state to distance itself from religion. On the contrary, the state in India plays an active role in managing religious affairs. Consequently, the Indian state is not secular in the formal sense of the term, unlike, say, the US or France, as discussed later in the book.

India's first prime minister was undoubtedly committed to the principle of secularism, as it is formally understood. But under the influence of Gandhi, who was tolerance personified but not 'secular' in the conventional sense, Nehru allowed the principle to be diluted in implementation. Secularism came to be regarded in India as a synonym for tolerance or pluralism, not as a doctrine to keep religion and state apart. Consequently, the concept became nebulous and began to mean all things to all people. Today, Hindu nationalist groups use the term 'pseudo-secular' to mock those who stand for tolerance or any spirit of accommodation towards minorities, even though these groups themselves are far from secular in their ideology.

Indian secularism raises problems of concept, interpretation, and, inevitably, of practice. If we place Indian secularism in the historical framework of secularism as an idea, we can argue that it is quite a case apart. The concept, as universally and historically understood, is different from its Indian incarnation, where tolerance of all religions, rather than a separation of religious affairs from those of the state, is the guiding principle. This often leads to a propensity to accommodate conflicting demands of competing religious groups in order to maintain public order.

Because of the violently divisive circumstances in which the Indian republic was born, the nation's early political leaders seem to have deliberately opted for an interpretation of secularism which was necessarily accommodative of a variety of religious opinions and demands. The government is thus compelled to ensure respect for India's diversity through a special interpretation of secularism. This, however, brings upon it the responsibility of protecting the particular identities of each of the numerous contending groups. One result is the rise of identity politics, in which India's many communities use a perceived softness of the state in religious matters to mobilize political power. In such a situation, tolerance tends to be eclipsed by a sense of communal identity, and that frequently leads to violent outcomes. Thus, India's well-intentioned, state-supported tolerance ends up generating intolerance.

In many ways, India's interpretation of secularism is not all that different from certain interpretations of Hinduism, particularly of the Gandhian variety. Gandhi was an apostle of tolerance, a great protestant reformer, and ahimsa was his ideology. He was nonetheless a Hindu literally to his last breath, who could effortlessly fit his ideology of nonviolence into a framework of universal tolerance that was compatible with his religious world-view. In his view, Hinduism was an accommodating religion, which accepted various ways of reaching the divine spirit, and called himself a *sanatani* Hindu. He not only made the Bhagavad Gita a central text of his version of Hinduism but saw a universalism in Hindu scriptures such as the Vedas. In his interpretation, Hinduism was a universal religion, tolerant and pluralist and ready to provide a spiritual home to adherents of all faiths. Not all faiths were ready to accept that; certainly not the Muslims, nor the Christians, who each had their own religious path to universal truth.

Gandhi wrote in his magazine *Young India* in May 1920:

> Let me explain what I mean by religion. It is not the Hindu religion, which I certainly prize over all other religions, but the religion which transcends Hinduism, which changes one's very nature, which binds one indissolubly to the truth within and which even purifies.

It was indeed his effort to go beyond common interpretations of Hinduism and make it acceptable to a range of groups, many of whom were in the lowest castes within the so-called Hindu fold. Other religious groups inevitably saw it as soft Hinduism.

Nevertheless, it influenced India's nationalist leaders, especially Nehru, who probably thought it prudent, given India's deep religiosity and the challenge he faced from the conservative Hindu nationalists on his right, to go along with

Gandhi's soft Hindu ideology and make it India's unique interpretation of secularism.

As it is commonly understood, secularism has nothing against private religiosity or the individual pursuit of religion. It is a creed that stands for the separation of church and state. It does not support any form of organized religion and has been historically locked in combat with religious power. It does not permit the use of public resources, such as government funds or state-held property, for religious use.

On a broader plane, secularism has historically involved an attempt to establish an autonomous sphere of knowledge devoid of supernatural, apocalyptic, and faith-based presuppositions. In the Middle Ages in Europe, a group of monks known as the Scholastics were probably the first to draw a distinction between faith and knowledge. All doctrines of faith are permeated with contradictions, which reason cannot accept, they asserted. Reason could operate only through resort to verifiable experience and not by reference to any supernatural world.

Gradually, over time, the growth and spread of capitalism helped establish secular power as distinct from ecclesiastical power. In the philosophical sphere, secularism is against theological or metaphysical absolutes; in the political sphere, it involves a separation of religious activity from political life and the establishment of the state as an independent source of power.

In India, the state, far from fighting for a separate identity, frequently caves in to accommodate demands made by religious groups, especially those that have acquired a political base. Government resources are often used for religious purposes. The state makes laws for religious denominations, and in some places administers religious institutions. While the soft character of Indian secularism can appear accommodating, it also creates inter-communal tension and resentment.

Three

THE POLITICS OF HATE

One evening in the early 1990s, an after-dinner conversation at a friend's house in Kolkata took an unpleasant turn after Mahatma Gandhi's name cropped up in a context I cannot recall. A man declared that he hated Gandhi and had been delighted that Nathuram Godse had assassinated him in 1948. An argument began between those who supported the man's view and others who were shocked that someone could feel happy, so many years after the event, at the murder of a nonviolent man widely regarded as the Father of the Nation. Feelings ran high well into the night.

The central complaint of the Gandhi-haters was that he had 'pampered' the Muslims of undivided India. The view was no different from Godse's own. When he had been tried and sentenced to death, Godse declared that the reason for the assassination was Gandhi's 'constant and consistent pandering to Muslims'. That feeling of intolerant resentment never died down; in fact, it intensified periodically in the decades following independence. A section of the population believes that Muslims have no place in India after Partition and that any idea of the nation based on pluralism or tolerance amounts to a woolly-headed appeasement of Muslims. Now it is true that Muslims in India have often used their minority status conspicuously to define the community as a separate entity deserving of special treatment in a secular land. However, the primary argument about how to define the Indian nation takes place within the majority community, and has periodically flared into violence.

Apart from this major source of dispute leading to intolerant behaviour, there are at least three other serious problem areas – inter-ethnic and inter-caste tensions, regional identity politics, and armed extremist movements – which continue to stir primordial feelings of hatred in the country. There are other areas of concern, such as the way women are still treated and a resultant worsening of the male to female ratio in the population; and increasing instances of rage in settling disagreements – from road rage to unparliamentary behaviour. However, communal antagonism between Hindus and Muslims is a core point of friction in a nation that was created to demonstrate the practical viability of the slogan 'unity in diversity'.

Communal massacres took place at the birth of the nation. Sporadic and less disastrous riots continued to erupt between Hindus and Muslims in various parts of the country through the following decades. But it was not before the end of the 1980s and the early 1990s that the ideology of Hindutva became a political force that its adherents could use to credibly aspire to national power. Such a resurrection of political Hinduism happened thanks to a move by the BJP to ally openly with hardline Hindu groups like the RSS and the Vishwa Hindu Parishad (VHP) in order to spread the gospel of Hindutva; and the alliance coalesced around an old dispute over a mosque.

That an innocuous plot of land, with a shrine on it, would assume such enormous portent in modern India's history was little anticipated by political observers in 1984, when the VHP revived a three-decade-old dispute over the origin of the shrine. An old mosque, the Babri Masjid, erected by a general in the army of Mughal emperor Babur in 1528, stood on the spot in Ayodhya in Uttar Pradesh. Hindus believed, however, that the general had built the mosque after demolishing a temple that had stood on the spot from at least the eleventh century CE to commemorate the birthplace of Ram, hero of the epic Ramayana. Whether it was indeed the birthplace of Ram was not an issue that provoked bitter dispute; whether a temple had been destroyed to build a mosque was the proverbial spark that lit the fire to blaze a track for the rise of Hindutva.

Secular scholars who have examined the issue broadly agree that the dispute between Hindus and Muslims over the site probably began in the mid-nineteenth century. Some historians blame the British for cynically exploiting a fraught situation to imperial advantage but they acknowledge that Hindus and Muslims may have begun quarrelling over the site some years before the British could intervene one way or another. Writing in *Anatomy of a Confrontation*, Sushil Srivastava of Allahabad University, for example, chastises the British for exploiting, around the time of the revolt of 1857, existing Hindu-Muslim differences over the Ram Janmabhoomi-Babri Masjid dispute. But he dates the dispute as having begun before the arrival of the British in the Avadh region, where Ayodhya is located, and suggests that the controversy might have been the result of a Hindu revival following the translation of the Ramayana into a popularly accessible form.

'It is quite clear,' writes Srivastava, 'that before and after the Revolt of 1857 the British Government encouraged Hindu activity. But it cannot be overlooked that Hindu revivalism had started spreading in Ayodhya much before the arrival of the British in Avadh.' British writers, he goes on, accepted that the emergence of Ayodhya as an important religious place among the Hindus was a modern phenomenon. 'We can agree,' he added, 'that the rendering of the Ramayana in the local dialect in the form of Ramcharitmanas helped in projecting Ram as the most popular avatar of Vishnu and a deity in North India.' This, he continues, led to the emergence of sects associated with the bhakti of Ram, and 'Ayodhya naturally became the main centre of their activity.'

Bloody clashes occurred between Hindus and Muslims over the site between 1853 and 1856. By that time, an idea had developed in the region that Babur had destroyed a Ram temple and erected a mosque in its place. In 1838, says Srivastava, British author Montgomery Martin wrote that the people of Ayodhya maintained that a mosque had been raised by Babur. Martin added that, as in other parts of India, in Ayodhya too Aurangzeb was blamed for the destruction of many Hindu temples. 'However, it was Babur's mosque that attracted Martin's attention most. He wrote that in the construction of the mosque, carved black stone pillars had been used and as they were un-Islamic they confirm the destruction of temples by Muslim zealots.'

Before 1857, Hindus and Muslims used to worship together at the mosque-temple site, according to W.C. Benet, writing in the *Gazetteer of the Province of Oudh*. After 1859, the British administrators concluded that hostile relations between Hindus and Muslims there required preventive measures. They therefore erected a fence to separate the places of worship of the two communities. Hindus could pray on a raised platform outside the mosque while Muslims could pray inside the mosque, both communities entering the site through different gates.

Thus it remained till the time of India's independence in 1947. When Hindus and Muslims began massacring one another across much of north India during the riots following Partition, the new government of India placed a guard outside the site and declared it out of bounds for both communities. Then, in December 1949, an image of Ram suddenly appeared in the mosque, apparently placed there one night by Hindu activists, and a rumour spread that Ram himself had arrived to claim the mosque as his temple. Riots broke out, and the army had to be called out to restore peace. The site stayed locked out for both communities, but the image of Ram remained inside. Although Muslim and Hindu leaders filed lawsuits claiming the site, no violent disturbance occurred there over the next four decades.

In 1984, the VHP raised a demand for the lock to be opened. Processions and rallies were organized in Ayodhya, Lucknow and Delhi in support of the demand but the assassination of Prime Minister Indira Gandhi in late 1984 and the subsequent general election diverted national attention away from the VHP's efforts. The VHP, however, continued its campaign, both politically and legally. In February 1986 a judge in Faizabad, not far from Ayodhya, ruled that the disputed site should be opened to the public. Riots broke out in north India; Muslims organized a huge protest in Delhi. Soon, the BJP, in coordination with the VHP with which it in any case had close familial ties, began moving the temple-mosque controversy towards the centre of national politics.

The BJP had not done well at all in the 1984 election in the wake of Indira Gandhi's murder – it could win just two of the 543 seats in Parliament against the Congress party's tally of 411 – and saw the temple-mosque issue as a rallying point for mobilization of Hindu support. In the 1989 general election, the BJP's tally rose to eighty-six seats with a vote share of just over 11 per cent. From then on, the party's rise to national prominence in the 1990s was rapid and it owed its success to the tactic of making the Babri Masjid-Ram Janmabhoomi issue a battle cry. By the end of the decade, the BJP became a formidable force on the national political stage. In the 1998 general election, the party won 180 parliamentary seats; its vote share rose to a quarter of the voting electorate; it formed the government with the help of allies and soon called for another election. It won again in 1999, with nearly the same vote share, and with 182 Lok Sabha seats, once more led the ruling coalition of parties.

Its road to success was marked by intolerance, which periodically led to outright violence. It was not a path strewn with the flowers of patience and accommodation which Hindu ideology, according to its advocates, was supposed to abide by. It was a bloody road that aimed to cut through the very idea of India.

In September 1989, the VHP began worshipping bricks, supposedly of Lord Ram's making, all across north India, with the aim of bringing them to the site in Ayodhya in order to build a temple displacing the Babri mosque. In the process, at least 300 people died, some of them kar sevaks, as the brick-bearing volunteers called themselves, and many Muslims perished in riots that followed some of the brick-carrying processions in north India. The kar sevaks succeeded in laying the stones outside the Babri mosque, but that was not the end of the story.

When V.P. Singh became prime minister of a National Front government following the 1989 general election, the BJP, with eighty-six MPs, decided to back him. In August 1990, the government decided to implement the report of the B. P. Mandal Commission, which had recommended a vastly expanded scheme of job reservations, and this move placed the BJP in an awkward position. The Mandal report had recommended a massive increase in job reservations for 'backward' castes in government service and educational institutions. Anti-reservation riots broke out and some upper-caste students went to the extent of immolating themselves. Hindu society seemed badly divided. What should the BJP do? Support the Mandal report or oppose it?

In the event, the party's leaders engineered a feint, deciding to take the debate back towards the temple-mosque issue. They announced a march, from the ancient Somnath temple in Gujarat to Ayodhya in Uttar Pradesh. Lal Krishna Advani would lead the march atop a Toyota truck modified to resemble Ram's chariot. He would halt many times along the way to address public meetings urging people to build the temple in Ayodhya. Advani posed on the truck with bow and arrow in hand, trying his elderly best to resemble Ram, while members of the VHP and Bajrang Dal offered him a cup of blood to demonstrate their determination to erect the temple in Ayodhya.

In speeches along the route, Advani accused the Union government of appeasing Muslims and practising 'pseudo-secularism', which, he said, denied the Hindu majority of the ability to fulfil their aspirations, and how building the temple was necessary to meet these.

The government of V. P. Singh was at a loss as to what to do. Opposing a march in support of Ram would be disastrous for his government because it would surely fall with the withdrawal of support by the BJP; yet an explosion was building up ahead if the marchers indeed entered Ayodhya on 30 October as planned, and began erecting a temple to replace the mosque. Advani and his entourage reached Delhi to camp for several days and the Union government did nothing to dissuade him.

A week before the march was to reach Ayodhya, however,

the Bihar government of Lalu Prasad Yadav placed Advani under preventive detention when the march entered the state. That did nothing to stop the marchers. While Advani remained confined in a Bihar government guesthouse, thousands of kar sevaks marched on to Ayodhya. The chief minister of Uttar Pradesh, Mulayam Singh Yadav, ordered the arrest of many, but thousands continued to march. On the morning of 30 October, a battle broke out between the marchers and the security forces, thousands of whom had been deployed in Ayodhya by the state government. The fight lasted three days; at least twenty kar sevaks died. Ashes from their cremated bodies were taken in urns around towns in north India and Hindus were urged by the VHP activists to take revenge. Inevitably, Hindu-Muslim riots broke out in Uttar Pradesh and hundreds more perished. Advani's march thus ended in widespread bloodshed.

The BJP withdrew support from the Union government and V. P. Singh resigned as prime minister in November 1990. In the general election that followed in the summer of 1991, the Congress won 244 seats, sufficient to form an alliance led by P. V. Narasimha Rao as prime minister (Rajiv Gandhi had been assassinated by a Sri Lankan Tamil terrorist). The BJP impressively increased its tally of seats in the Lok Sabha from eighty-six to 120 and formed the state government in Uttar Pradesh. The party was now a serious contender for future national power. Ram was delivering votes.

Meanwhile, the VHP was determined to keep the temple-mosque controversy on the boil. In October 1991, its volunteers began readying the ground around the mosque as a prelude to building a temple. The Narasimha Rao government, sensing trouble, tried to get the two principal contestants, the VHP and the Babri Masjid Action Committee, to discuss the issue and negotiate a settlement, but to no avail.

The VHP announced 6 December 1992 as the day when it would begin building the temple. It assumed that with a BJP government in power in Uttar Pradesh it had little to fear in terms of legal or administrative constraint. It was right.

Around mid-November, volunteers for temple construction began pouring into Ayodhya. The BJP state government, under chief minister Kalyan Singh, provided them with food and housing even as a nervous Union government, led by the Congress, began sending paramilitary forces to the area. Tensions ran high as, by the end of the month, 20,000 paramilitary troops and over one lakh kar sevaks, armed with bows, arrows and tridents, descended on the small town.

On 6 December, the announced day of reckoning, the state government sent its own police force to guard the troubled spot while Central paramilitary forces awaited orders some distance away. As crowds of kar sevaks moved menacingly towards the mosque in the morning, the police first tried to stop them and then fled. Without tracing the events of the fateful day, on which volumes have been written, we can note that by the late afternoon, the volunteers had reduced the mosque to rubble.

There was some hand-wringing in the top leadership of the BJP after the mosque's demolition. For instance, when RSS chief K.S. Sudarshan asked Advani to accept what had happened as the deed had been done, the latter replied that he would publicly express his regret. It was, however, the hatred he had unleashed and abetted in the first place that had led to an outcome about which he now wanted to express regret.

Riots broke out all over northern and western India following the destruction at Ayodhya. Volunteers moved from the site after demolishing the mosque to set a few Muslim homes on fire. In other places, the VHP organized triumphant processions, which provoked rioting. Mumbai, in particular, was badly hit after the Shiv Sena and the BJP called a strike in protest against the arrest of some of their men in Ayodhya. The army had to be called out to restore peace, which held for a short while before dissolving into rioting in January. At least 800 died in Mumbai, most of them Muslim.

On 12 March 1993, some underworld dons of the Muslim community sought revenge by planting a string of bombs all over the city of Mumbai, with one explosion paralysing the stock exchange. At least 300 died in the blasts. One of the masterminds of the bombings, Dawood Ibrahim, remains at large in Dubai and Pakistan. Thus, communal politics surrounding a shrine in a small town in Uttar Pradesh had torn to shreds the famed fabric of tolerance of India's leading commercial metropolis and sullied its cosmopolitan reputation.

This did not, however, affect the BJP's political fortunes. In the next general election, in late 1996, it became the largest single party in Parliament with a tally of 161 seats. It tried to put together a government but failed after two weeks of effort. A rag-tag bunch of parties formed the national government while the BJP waited on the opposition benches. In 1998, it came back in contention after a mid-term general election by securing 182 seats and formed the government. A year later, its prime minister, Atal Behari Vajpayee, called another election and the party again won 182 seats, with the Congress tally sinking to an all-time low of 114. Vajpayee led a coalition government that stayed in power for a full term of five years.

The march of Hindutva continued. While BJP leaders in Delhi, including the moderate-sounding Vajpayee, offered verbal assurances that the construction of a Ram temple at Ayodhya, in place of the Babri mosque, would happen, the VHP went about organizing the momentum necessary for the exercise. Volunteers from elsewhere in the country were taken on tours of Ayodhya, and religious ceremonies were held in preparation for the construction.

In February 2002, one group of volunteers from Gujarat was on its way back when the train carrying them stopped at the Godhra railway station. It was a town in Gujarat with a sizeable Muslim population and a history of communal tension. Reportedly, some volunteers alighted from the train and got into an argument with some Muslim vendors at the station platform. They apparently asked the Muslims to recite Hindu slogans, which the vendors refused. This soon led to a growing altercation, which was joined by Muslim youth from the neighbourhood. The kar sevaks reboarded the train as it restarted amidst stone throwing. However, when a fire broke out in one of the carriages, the train stopped again outside the station. Fifty-eight persons were burnt alive in that fire, the origin of which has never been fully established. The VHP alleged that the train was set alight by the Muslim mob. Their word spread rapidly through the state and, it seems, across the world, as we mentioned in the opening chapter. Riots engulfed the entire state of Gujarat.

Over 2,000 died, most of them Muslim; at least 100,000 became homeless. The BJP chief minister of the state, an RSS-nurtured ideologue named Narendra Modi, said the violence was an outcome of the burning of the train carriage in Godhra, a 'chain of action and reaction'. In fact, as later reports revealed, the mobs doing the killing and burning were led by VHP activists who were assisted in turn by members of the local administrations of Gujarat's towns and villages. The rioters carried voters' lists to help them identify Muslim homes. The police allegedly gave a free hand to the VHP and Bajrang Dal as they went about systematically massacring Muslims, raping women, killing children, and burning neighbourhoods.

Narendra Modi was re-elected to power in Gujarat not once but twice after this, in late 2002 and, after a five-year term in power, in late 2007. The ideology of Hindutva, it seemed, was on a relentless march. Yet that was not the reality.

The sway of the BJP over India's voters had possibly reached a plateau, as recent elections have suggested. Its national support base failed to go beyond a band of between 20 and 25 per cent of the voting electorate. If anything, after its defeat in the 2009 general election, the BJP's position declined sharply, with, losses in a number of state elections, and with its leadership in apparent disarray.

In the 2004 general election, the BJP yielded power to a Congress-led United Progressive Alliance (UPA). Since its vote share had stayed roughly the same as in the previous election, it could be assumed that the BJP lost because it had not struck the right alliances with regional parties. That fact, however, also suggests that by itself the party had not expanded its support base after six years in power at the centre. Its route to power, like that of the Congress, lay through alliances with regional parties, none of which, apart from the Shiv Sena in Maharashtra, shared its ideology of Hindutva.

The 2009 general election results were more dismal for the BJP. Its vote share showed a decline; its number of seats in the Lok Sabha fell from 138 in 2004 to 121. The Congress did remarkably well by capturing 206 Lok Sabha seats, up from 145 in 2004, and once again formed a coalition government under the leadership of Manmohan Singh as prime minister. Although the BJP was still in control of a few state governments, its performance in the general election across the board was poor. In Uttar Pradesh, where Ayodhya is located, it campaigned hard but performed poorly; it had apparently lost its ideological appeal.

Its performance in Uttar Pradesh in the 2009 general election is a good starting point for examining what went wrong with the BJP's appeal. After all, that was the base camp from which it had begun its phenomenal climb in the 1990s. If we frame the picture in the contrasting styles and personalities of two prominent cousins, who fought the election on rival platforms, it may help us understand what happened. Rahul Gandhi, son of Sonia Gandhi, the Congress president, and the late Rajiv Gandhi, campaigned for the Congress. Varun Gandhi, son of Maneka Gandhi and the late Sanjay Gandhi, Rajiv's brother, campaigned for the BJP.

Varun's approach was aggressive, full of burning saffron rage. He taunted Muslims and goaded people into being conscious of identities in ethnic, caste, and communal colours. Rahul's way was to project a quiet image of a young politician who wanted to get on with the job while keeping his party's goal in steady focus. Varun loudly wanted vengeance for imagined and real grievances; Rahul calmly exuded tolerance.

Varun spoke the language of the Hindutva ideologue: India's majority must consolidate its group identity into 'us' and 'them' and build a masculine, muscular nation – the kind that Ram the warrior king represented during his glorious, ancient reign. A monolithic majority would rule the nation, and would perhaps even be charitable to Muslims, so long as they fell in line with the dominant Hindu ethos. Minorities would be generously treated if they didn't raise their voices.

Rahul, by contrast, appeared almost indifferent to the politics of identity. He did not seem to believe in a singular idea of a majority community that could coalesce into a force to build Ram Rajya in this day and age. He reflected a secular view of India. In this view, all citizens of a secular democracy belong to one minority or the other; only Indians are recognized by the Constitution as a collective but diverse entity. It is a salad bowl in which various individualities and identities can mingle; it is unwise to turn it into a melting pot of steely nationalism defined by any particular religion.

Rahul's approach worked, the Congress did better than expected in Uttar Pradesh; Varun's tactics backfired on the BJP. But will it be able to draw the correct lesson? Is the

BJP capable of adjusting its ideology to the evolving need of the times? Or is it structurally incapable of incorporating ideological adjustments because of its ties with the RSS?

The BJP is not an autonomously born political party but the political arm of the RSS. Elected to power and leading a diverse coalition, the BJP has to make compromises to suit the reality of India's politics. Its leaders can promise while campaigning that a temple will be built in Ayodhya; once in power it has to find creative ways out of that promise. In fact, the way a BJP-led coalition ruled India for six years was not fundamentally different from the way Congress-led governments conduct affairs of the state and politics. It can hardly be otherwise. Major decisive moves have to be made after careful deliberation, with one eye on electoral viability and the other on the feasibility of any move given the compulsions of coalition governments.

That is not how the RSS sees it. It can afford to maintain ideological purity because it does not have to exercise executive authority in a tricky political environment. It doesn't even admit that it is a political organization; its leaders insist it is nothing but a cultural and social outfit. Even so, it dictates the course of the BJP's actions, often micromanaging the party's business, from selection of candidates for election to the appointment of national leaders. The RSS is the BJP's father and a very stern one indeed.

I use the term 'father' deliberately, rather than 'parent' or 'mother'. The mythology of Hinduism created by the RSS is a masculine one in which aggression and anger are qualities of manhood to be preferred over any effeminate quality such as tolerance. Leaders of the RSS and the BJP like to model themselves on Ram, the warrior-king, whose masculine powers make him a 'maryada purushottam', or supreme man. Thus L.K. Advani's image was built up as an ideal 'lauh purush', or iron man, who could bring glory to the nation through manly leadership that would brush out of its way the weakness and debilitating passivity of effeminate secularists. The fact that the Indian electorate brushed him aside in two successive general elections did not make a dent in the masculine orientation of the RSS leadership. They probably saw it as a sign of insufficient masculinity in an aged leader rather than any defect in an ideology that prized exclusivist aggression over tolerance in a multicultural nation.

The RSS was founded on the exclusivist beliefs of its founder, K.B. Hedgewar, that India was a Hindu nation and that all other inhabitants were either foreigners or those who had been misled by foreigners into other faiths. Walter Andersen and Shridhar Damle note in their book *Brotherhood in Saffron: The Rashtriya Swayamsevak Sangh and Hindu Revivalism*, that in September 1925, after founding the organization in Nagpur, Hedgewar began to develop the intellectual foundations of the RSS. A major influence on his thinking was a handwritten manuscript of (V.D.) Savarkar. The central propositions of Savarkar's manuscript were that Hindus were the indigenous people of the subcontinent and that they formed a single national group.

The ideological guru of the RSS was Hedgewar's successor as the head of the organization, Madhav Sadashiv Golwalkar. He is spoken of in reverential terms in the Sangh fraternity as Guru Golwalkar. In his 1939 treatise, *We Or Our Nationhood Defined*, he wrote that the 'foreign races in Hindusthan' must adopt Hindu culture and language, must learn to respect and hold in reverence the Hindu religion, must entertain no ideas but those of the glorification of the Hindu race and culture, and must lose their separate existence to merge in the Hindu race. Or, they might stay in the country 'wholly subordinated to the Hindu nation, claiming nothing, deserving no privileges, far less any preferential treatment, not even citizen's rights.' He added: 'We are an old nation; let us deal, as old nations ought to and do deal, with the foreign races who have chosen to live in our country.'

Golwalkar believed that 'in Hindusthan, religion is an all-absorbing entity. Based as it is on the unshakeable foundations of a sound philosophy of life... it has become eternally woven into the life of the Race and forms, as it were, its very Soul.' He was, consequently, harsh on Gandhi's advocacy of secular nationalism. He disparaged the idea that the nation was composed of all those who happened to reside therein and that these people were to unite on a common 'national' platform and win back freedom by 'Constitutional means'. He felt that 'wrong notions of democracy strengthened the view and we began to class ourselves with our old invaders and foes under the outlandish name – Indian – and tried to win them over to join hands with us in our struggle'.

Democracy for Golwalkar was 'to a very large extent a myth in practice' and the 'high sounding concept of individual freedom only meant the freedom of the talented few to exploit the rest'. In a speech in 1960, he called Muslims, Jews, Christians and Parsis 'guests' who are not children of the soil. About India's Constitution, he wrote, in *Why Hindu Rashtra*: 'Unfortunately in our country our Constitution has equated the children of the soil with the aggressor and given equal rights to everybody, just as a person without understanding may give equal rights to his children and to the thieves in his house and distribute the property among all.'

The BJP today is hostage to a world-view founded on such archaic intolerance, which goes against the Constitution of India. Yet the party has to swear by that very document when it fights its political battles or is thrust into governing an India the very name of which was distasteful to the leading ideologue of the RSS. There is space in the political spectrum for a conservative party in India, not a culturally regressive party but one that has come to terms with the idea of India as enshrined in the Constitution. Such a party can, for instance, advocate slowing the pace of change and attempt to build an exceptional Indian identity by broadening the scope of cultural and social identification in order to accommodate the multifaceted reality of India.

But will the BJP take the risk? Actually, can it, unless it is ready to distance itself from the RSS, its intellectual parent and political master? For that to happen, the BJP will have to develop a different world-view; one rooted not in the myths of the past but on an acceptance of the diversity of India and the imperatives of modern development. Alternatively, the RSS will have to reassess its ideological understanding of Indian reality and allow its political front, the BJP, full autonomy in matters of politics and governance by living up to its assertion that it is a social and cultural organization seeking to do good for Indian society, and that it has no interest in political power.

Four

DEMOCRACY, DYNASTY AND CONGRESS

On the first anniversary of India's independence, in a talk broadcast from New Delhi, Jawaharlal Nehru said:

> Let us be rid of everything that limits us and degrades us. Let us cast out fear and communalism and provincialism. Let us build up a free and democratic India… Democracy means tolerance, tolerance not merely of those who agree with us, but of those who do not agree with us. With the coming of freedom our patterns of behaviour must change also so as to fit in with this freedom.

How has the Congress party of Nehru and Gandhi lived up to that eloquent appeal? On the whole, better than those parties and groups that from the outset contested the idea of a multicultural and multiethnic India. But its record is patchy, with some distinct blots of both communalism and intolerance marring its canvas. It has, however, managed to remain committed to defending the founding idea of a secular India.

At the outset, the founding fathers formalized the concept of an India that would not be discriminatory towards any of its citizens but would be the world's newest, and perhaps unlikeliest, experiment in secular nation building. On 3 April 1948, the Constituent Assembly passed a resolution moved by the first Depury Speaker of the Lok Sabha, Ananthasayanam Ayangar:

> Whereas it is essential for the proper functioning of democracy and the growth of national unity and solidarity that communalism should be eliminated from Indian life, this Assembly is of opinion that no communal organization which, by its constitution or by the exercise of discretionary power vested in any of its officers or organs, admits to or excludes from its membership persons on grounds of religion, race and caste, or any of them should be permitted to engage in any activities other than those essential for the bonafide religious, cultural, social and educational needs of the community, and that all steps, legislative and administrative, necessary to prevent such activities should be taken.

That was about as clear a statement of secular intent on which the republic would be built as you would find anywhere in the early proceedings of the Constituent Assembly. Accepting the resolution on behalf of the government, Nehru said:

> … the combination of politics and of religion in the narrowest sense of the word, resulting in communal politics is, there can be no doubt, a most dangerous combination and must be put an end to.

Here it might be useful to reiterate a degree of difference between Gandhi's advocacy of nonviolence and tolerance, as preached during the nationalist movement, and Nehru's take on secularism in the formative stages of independent India. Gandhi's was a reinterpretation of Hinduism in a nonviolent, pluralist sense and was a spiritual construction of tolerance. Nehru's view, at least in those initial days, was a forthright desire to keep politics and religion apart and his outlook was clearly secular in the modern, universally accepted sense of the term.

From 1947 to 1967 the Congress was dominant in the Indian political system. In the first three general elections, in 1952,1957 and 1962, which coincided with elections to the state assemblies, the Congress won over two-thirds of the seats in the Lok Sabha, as well as a majority of seats in most states. The 1967 general election, however, proved to be a watershed in Indian politics. The Congress won only 283 seats in the Lok Sabha, just about enough to form the national government, and lost power in eight out of the sixteen state assemblies.

Through that entire period of success, the Congress was widely seen as the 'umbrella' party. It retained more characteristics of the movement that it was during the freedom struggle than of a political party. Unlike the Jan Sangh and the communist parties, it did not have a cadre-based organization; its rules of membership were flexible and virtually anyone could become a member by walking into its tent.

It housed a wide diversity of views and beliefs. It selected leaders at the state as well as the national level through regular party elections and encouraged the airing of different opinions within its fold. True, some felt that the overpowering personality of Nehru did not encourage the growth of other centres of leadership. But there was enough variety in the party, both in centres of power as well as in ideas.

There were Nehruvian socialists and liberal free-market advocates. They were all broadly secular in their outlook but many had pronounced Hindu nationalist leanings. Some believed in a strong, centralized governing structure for India, others were in favour of decentralization. In internal party conflicts over ideology, a process of bargaining and reconciliation worked by and large successfully towards creating a consensus at the national level.

In those days of freshly flowered freedom, consensus was relatively easy to create. At the helm of affairs was the towering figure of Jawaharlal Nehru, who had enormous nationwide popularity and the vision as well as leadership skills to forge a consensus on matters of public policy. His hold over the party weakened after the debacle of the 1962 border war with China and he passed away in May 1964. Nonetheless, the succession to leadership after his death was smooth.

The Congress style of functioning was democratic, internally and externally. By being in power so long, it had also amassed sufficient financial resources to offer patronage when required and aspiring politicians found it a convenient platform to ascend. The party adapted its tactics to suit local conditions and attracted local leaders to join it. While its major campaign funds came from industrial houses, which were with the party through the freedom movement, and from sections of rich farmers and landowners, it would be difficult to identify any single elite as dominating the party. Each state and district produced its own kind of leadership while the party continued to keep its door open to a widening pool of social groups.

Problems began to arise when a succession struggle began following the unexpected death in 1966 of Lal Bahadur Shastri, Nehru's successor. A tussle for the leadership ended in Indira Gandhi being selected by party managers, the so-called Syndicate, as prime minister, not because she was an exceptional candidate but because she was considered innocuous and easier to manipulate than her rival Morarji Desai. Thus began the reign of one of the most transformative figures in Indian politics. Her leadership style and convictions had a huge impact on the direction India forged while the Congress party changed from an umbrella organization to a family fief.

The Syndicate had clearly underestimated Indira Gandhi. The details of how she assumed control over the party are well known and have been recorded and analysed by several historians and political scientists. She split the party in 1969 and, with the support of the communist parties, retained a parliamentary majority. One of her early acts was to use that majority to abolish political contributions from industry; this in effect squeezed the flow of funds to parties and politicians out of power, including the Syndicate-led section of the Congress, while she continued to generate unaccounted funds from industry by using the levers of the so-called Licence-Permit Raj. She nationalized major commercial banks as well as insurance companies and shipping lines, which helped further consolidate her power.

With a sharp sense of political timing she announced a mid-term general election in 1971. For the first time since independence, national and provincial elections were delinked and she led a vigorous national campaign on the slogan 'Garibi Hatao' (abolish poverty). She was thus able to successfully portray her opponents – including the old Syndicate-led Congress and the up-and-coming liberal Swatantra Party – as pro-rich and her wing of the Congress as the party of the poor. The communists, who were ranged against the Congress in West Bengal and Kerala, were supporting her in Parliament and were thus not in any position to counter her pro-poor rhetoric.

The Indira Congress won a two-thirds majority in the Lok Sabha in 1971 and swept the state assembly elections the year after. 'India is Indira and Indira is India,' crowed the sycophantic president of the Congress, Dev Kanta Borooah, and with it began the personalization of politics. The Congress of Indira Gandhi became more and more centralized, especially after she did away with inner-party democracy by dropping the process of holding internal party elections. Through charismatic leadership, the credibility of which was boosted to a great extent by a victory over Pakistan in the 1971 Bangladesh war, Indira Gandhi went about centralizing control over the party and ruled the nation largely with the guidance of a coterie of advisers.

While Jawaharlal Nehru understood the true nature of India well, not so his daughter. Despite occasional flashes of an authoritarian streak in his personality, Nehru was a democrat to the core. He respected the Opposition and treated members of other parties with extreme civility. He observed parliamentary norms and encouraged the growth of a free press. He kept alive inner-party democracy within the Congress, consciously kept the judiciary independent and the bureaucracy autonomous.

His daughter, by contrast, followed her father's footsteps only casually, if at all. Although a superb tactician with a tremendous acumen for political timing, her innate tendency, it seemed to many who came to know her closely, was not to trust anyone outside her innermost, devotedly loyal circle.

The liberal-minded, big-tent party of Mohandas Gandhi and Jawaharlal Nehru soon became a family-led enterprise. The process became obvious during the infamous state of Emergency, which Indira Gandhi declared in June 1975, when she faced the threat of being unseated by an admittedly trivial court decision over electoral propriety. Her reaction to the threat was to muzzle the press, throw opponents into jail, and rule India for nineteen months without any pretension to democratic formality.

That was the period when the Congress, which had already become a centralized, personality-based power structure, rapidly turned into a dynastic apparatus. It is pertinent to point out here that Indira Gandhi's own rise to the prime minister's job was not a dynastic succession. It was Lal Bahadur Shastri's sudden death that forced the Congress to select a leader and the party managers chose her for convenience. This was not the case with the rise, initially, of her younger son, Sanjay, and then her older son, Rajiv.

Sanjay initially took charge of the party's youth wing and was then put in charge of the capital city of Delhi. He offered a five-point plan for the nation: urgent family planning, planting trees nationwide to revive forests, banning the dowry system, eradicating illiteracy, and clearing urban slums. Of these, he put special emphasis on family planning nationally and slum clearance in the Delhi metropolitan area. With the help of Jagmohan, the vice chairman of the Delhi Development Authority, and sundry personal friends and acolytes, he went about demolishing slums in Delhi. During the fifteen years before he launched his drive, the DDA had removed 60,000 families from the slums of the city; during the fifteen months of the Emergency when Sanjay Gandhi went about the task with zeal, over twice that number were evicted.

Although the press was barred from reporting a word, matters came to a head at the Turkman Gate area of the city in April 1976. With bulldozers in action, the DDA officials went about demolishing houses. After a few days, residents of the area came out in protest, with even women and children standing up to block bulldozers. The police first used tear gas and lathis to break up the protests; when that didn't work, they fired. No one knows for sure how many succumbed to the bullets, because it all happened without media coverage.

Sanjay's approach to family planning was based on a similar style of an ill-informed and intolerant notion of efficiency before all else. It was, and remains, a common attitude in sections of the urban middle class in India; an assumption that problems of nation building are not at all complex if you are ruthlessly disciplined and ready to shed blood, if necessary, in the single-minded pursuit of rapid, orderly growth.

When touring India, Sanjay would set family planning targets for chief ministers, urging them to exceed the set goals in competition with one another. District officials were required to carry out the task, and would be either rewarded or transferred from their postings depending on how they performed. Inevitably in such circumstances, coercion became widespread, especially in the towns of north India. Soon, compulsory sterilizations began of men who had three or more children. People refused and rose in protest in some parts of the country, again without such resistance being reported in the press. Violence broke out in several towns; in Muzaffarnagar, near Delhi, over fifty people died in police firing.

A personal idol of mine, the singer-actor Kishore Kumar, refused to perform on Sanjay Gandhi's orders to raise money for sterilizations. As a consequence, his songs were banned from Vividh Bharati, the radio channel that broadcast film music. The film censor board held up the release of movies in which Kishore Kumar acted or sang. Sanjay's men also warned record companies against selling his songs.

Thus, within a relatively short period of time, Indira Gandhi, in her quest to make the inheritance of power hereditary, allowed the destruction of the democratic tradition that her father had so carefully nurtured while leading the new Republic of India. For a while it seemed that the developing world's greatest experiment in democratic nation building had failed, like so many similar attempts elsewhere.

Indira Gandhi had inherited a reasonably unified nation. Not for her the doubts, the questioning and the search for answers that overlay her father's thinking. Her India was a less nuanced concept but was a reality nonetheless. Its unity was periodically threatened so it had to be maintained at all cost and she was, in her mind, the only person capable of preserving the idea. All her politics, therefore, had to be directed towards that singular goal of keeping India intact. In order to achieve that goal, she seemed to believe that she or her descendants had to retain full command. The Emergency was a logical outcome of that mindset.

Nehru was a liberal democrat in the European, some would say 'Anglo-Saxon', sense of the term and leant towards a mild form of socialism in his economic thinking. Indira Gandhi changed the preamble to the Constitution to include the word 'socialist' in order to make any divergent viewpoint unconstitutional. By nationalizing the banking industry, she assumed control of the pulleys of financial power in ways her father never attempted and her calls to socialism were instrumental in preparing the ground for more effective centralization of power.

However, to the surprise of many, in January 1977, Indira Gandhi announced a fresh general election. Precisely why she did so is not known, but it could have been a combination of factors, including persistent criticism abroad by old friends of India – some of them friends of the Nehru family – and an assessment by her intelligence bureau that she would win a general election hands down. All the reported reasons cited by historians suggest, however, that she was uncomfortable with the prospect of running India as a permanent dictatorship. She was also aware that growing factionalism within her party, especially in reaction to Sanjay's heavy-handed style, might make it difficult to sustain the state of Emergency for long. She must have thought that it would be better to go for a fresh mandate, and hoped for the kind of majority she had got in 1971.

That factionalism within the party was a growing problem was evident to many of us who were in journalism but were not allowed by the censors to report what was going on. As a young reporter, based in Calcutta, for the *Economic Times*, I had to prepare three copies of every article I wrote: one for the news editor, one for the censor's office in New Delhi, and one for the local censor who worked down the lane from our office in central Calcutta. That's how it was for the first year or so of the Emergency.

By mid-1976, it had become evident to us reporters that we could play games with the censors by setting one off against another. Every now and then, if the local office did not pass a story for its political content, we would call our Delhi office to see if the objection could be overruled and the article passed by the central censors. Or, vice versa. In the later months of the Emergency this ruse worked fine as the ruling Congress leaderships in Delhi and Calcutta did not see eye to eye on most matters.

Sanjay Gandhi had come to dislike West Bengal's chief minister, Siddhartha Sankar Ray, who had been Indira Gandhi's confidant when she had required legal advice in order to consolidate her Emergency rule. Ray, to his credit, had declined to become a sycophant of the son, unlike many other Congress leaders. The state Congress, as well as the local cabinet of ministers, were badly split over the quarrel. Though we could not directly write a word about it we began using it creatively.

Similar divisions had begun to appear in some other states. Even within the central party establishment, not everyone was prepared to bow before the heir apparent. In fact, the reality of the coalition that is India had begun to overtake Sanjay's and his mother's attempt to govern this diverse nation as a singular, disciplined unit. If the Emergency's failure to last proved one truth, it was that India would have to be governed in an accommodating and tolerant manner befitting its diversity.

Although the Congress was roundly defeated in the 1977 election, the party losing over 200 seats from its 1971 tally, it did reasonably well in the southern Indian states. In the northern states, it was almost wiped out, largely due to popular revulsion against Sanjay Gandhi's strong-arm methods of family planning. Thus ended the first phase of the decline of the Congress from a broadly liberal, democratic organization to an illiberal family-run enterprise.

The Janata coalition did not last long. In less than three years, during which two coalition governments tried to govern the nation from Delhi and made a hash of it, Indira Gandhi and Sanjay were back in power. Their desire to keep the party fully under their control entered a second phase of success. In the 1980 general election, the Congress won 353 seats in the Lok Sabha on the slogan that Janata could not hold a government together and that Indira Gandhi was India's saviour.

Sanjay now was a member of Parliament, as well as general secretary of the Congress party. He was clearly the chosen inheritor of his mother's mantle and the future leader of the party. This time around, dissension within the organization was non-existent; local leaders fell over one another in their efforts to ingratiate themselves with mother and son. Fate, however, intervened cruelly.

On 23 June 1980, Sanjay went flying in a single engine plane for fun, as he often did. While trying aerobatics, he lost control and died as the plane crashed. Indira Gandhi was shattered and became withdrawn for a while, but not for long. She soon turned to her elder son, Rajiv, to step into his late brother's shoes.

Before long, Rajiv was elected a member of Parliament. Senior leaders of the party began making a beeline to his door to pay their respects. The reluctant politician became a general secretary of the party and the new heir apparent to his mother.

The second reign of Indira Gandhi was a difficult one. An agitation for greater autonomy by Sikhs in Punjab developed into a major crisis that took up much of the attention of the Union government and eventually cost the prime minister her life.

Like several other communities in India, the Sikhs of Punjab had grievances against what they saw as excessive centralization of power in India. In 1973, the Sikh regional party, Akali Dal, had passed a resolution demanding autonomy for Punjab and a revised Constitution based on 'real federal principles'. That Anandpur Sahib Resolution lay dormant through much of the 1970s but was resurrected, with new demands added, after the Akali Dal won the state election in 1977. Around that time, a radical named Jarnail Singh Bhindranwale began militantly preaching that Sikhs were like slaves in India and should fight for their freedom.

To cut a long and complicated story short, the Punjab disturbance became a nightmare for the Union government. Nonviolent agitation and assassinations moved on parallel tracks. Negotiations for autonomy within the Indian system continued while demands for an independent 'Khalistan', largely supported by overseas Sikh communities, mounted as the extremists pushed moderates towards hardline positions. Relations between Hindus and Sikhs deteriorated sharply.

As violence escalated in Punjab, Bhindranwale holed up with a group of followers in the holiest of holy Sikh shrines, the Golden Temple in Amritsar. With assassinations being planned and carried out from within the temple, the Union government concluded that it had no option but to flush out the terrorists sheltering there. The army was called out and, in early June 1984, it waged a bloody battle with the extremists inside the temple in an exercise known as Operation Bluestar. At least 500 died in the battle, among them Bhindranwale.

The feelings of Sikhs everywhere were deeply hurt. The Golden Temple had been attacked and damaged under orders from a government led by Indira Gandhi. The prime minister was warned of a threat to her life, possibly from her own security personnel, which she brushed off. On 31 October 1984, two Sikh bodyguards shot her dead as she walked from her home to her office next door.

What followed etched a terrible dark mark in the Congress party's record of tolerance. Beginning with loot and arson on the night of the assassination, mobs went on the rampage, most horrifically in Delhi, murdering Sikhs, looting homes and shops, burning Sikh shrines and holy books. Over a thousand Sikhs died in Delhi in the two or three days of rioting. Congress activists, including elected politicians and ministers in many instances, led the mobs. The police did little to stop the rampage and in some places actively abetted the looting and burning.

Rajiv Gandhi, who had been expectedly sworn in as prime minister on the evening of 31 October, made a comment that showed an unfortunate lack of sensitivity. He said: 'When a big tree falls, the earth shakes.' He was doubtless distraught and was reflecting the anger of millions of his fellow countrymen who had been exasperated by the Sikh agitation and were infuriated by the murder of the prime minister. Now however, as the prime minister of the nation, he did not seem to appreciate that his first duty should have been to calm tempers and stop the bloodletting. Instead, he seemed to be suggesting that the law of the jungle could be allowed to prevail in some circumstances.

He went on to score a landslide victory in the general election that followed. He matured quickly as a political leader and led the Congress government for a full term of five years. He signed accords with dissident groups, including the Sikhs, and restored political stability. He tried to free the Indian economy from the shackles of a state-led growth pattern but interest groups both within his own party and outside thwarted his effort. The same happened when he tried to repair some of the damage caused to his party and the nation's institutions in his mother's reign. Towards the end of his term as prime minister, Rajiv Gandhi struggled to fend off charges of corruption involving the purchase of field guns for the armed forces from the Swedish firm Bofors. The Congress party lost the 1989 general election.

After the defeat of the Congress in the 1989 election, Rajiv Gandhi was assassinated by a Sri Lankan Tamil terrorist while he was campaigning in the next general election two years later. The Congress returned to lead a coalition in 1991 under the leadership of P. V. Narasimha Rao. With the country facing a balance of payments crisis, which forced the government to approach the International Monetary Fund and the World Bank for assistance, Rao and his finance minister, Manmohan Singh, let loose a quiet revolution in India's economic thinking. However, neither Rao, a careful manager with a bureaucratic mindset, nor anyone else could provide true political leadership to the Congress party, which had become a trusteeship of the Gandhi family, and no one from the family was ready at that time to take charge.

Rao's coalition completed five years in power and lost in 1996. The Congress remained out in the cold for eight years. In 2004, as the lead party in the United Progressive Alliance, it nosed ahead of the rival BJP-led National Democratic Alliance. With Manmohan Singh as prime minister and Rajiv's widow Sonia Gandhi in charge of the party, it completed a five-year term. It won again, impressively, in 2009, when it added sixty-one seats to its 2004 score to notch up 206 seats in the Lok Sabha.

The Congress party today appears to be in relatively better shape than it has been in the past quarter of a century, despite its record on corruption and in leading weak governments. Manmohan Singh, now into his second term, is India's first member of a minority community to head a national government. Having him as prime minister is a boon for Congress in several senses. As a Sikh leading the government, he has helped heal to some degree the scars of the anti-Sikh riots of 1984. His unflappable public demeanour, his personal humility, and his honesty add to his well-deserved reputation as the father of India's growth-inspiring economic reforms.

In running the party's affairs, Rajiv's widow Sonia Gandhi has demonstrated greater competence than her rivals in the BJP, while her thirty-nine-year-old son Rahul appears to be raising the hopes of a new generation of Indians. After the hollowing out of the party's internal structure under his grandmother, Rahul seems keen on restoring a semblance of democracy, at least at the lower levels, within the party. It would be too much to expect the Congress to return to its days of being the nation's political umbrella, but Rahul Gandhi seems intent on reviving the party's inclusive character. We can only hope that his intentions are genuine and that he will succeed despite basking in an atmosphere of persisting sycophancy. Unfortunately for him, the recent storm of charges of corruption against the government has placed the party once again in a corner while his and Sonia's image has also suffered.

Rahul Gandhi would do well to study the beliefs and style of functioning not of his grandmother but of his great-grandfather. He might replace Nehru's now outdated socialist wisdom with Manmohan Singh's progressive economic views; but he would do well to imbibe Nehru's informed and reasoned convictions on tolerance, liberalism and the spirit of live and let live that is so essential to democratic life.

Five

ISLAM AND INTOLERANCE

I grew up in a joint family home in a quiet neighbourhood of Calcutta. For us children in the family, it was fun all the way, especially during the festive season, starting from around late September to the end of the year. Schools were shut for four weeks during Durga Puja and another four during Christmas and New Year. That was our time for picnics and celebration. We went for rides around the city during Puja time, driven by the family chauffeur, Khaleq Babu. That's what we called him, taking a cue from our elders. He would traverse the entire town with us in tow. He took us to Puja funfairs while telling us tales of the goddess Durga and about Ram's return from banishment. He told us how a dacoit, Ratnakar, had been fascinated by Ram's tale and had written the Ramayana as Valmiki the sage. He told us about the prowess of Durga, who slew demons, and he described in detail how the goddess Kali emerged to drink the blood of monsters so that they could not rise.

That Khaleq Babu was a Muslim was a fact that had never occurred to me, or any of the other kids, until I was around nine or ten. It was when the family had assembled at the wedding of his son, Akram, at a house near Park Circus, that I asked my father why this wedding ceremony looked different from the way I had seen weddings performed at home, and why the food they had served was so deliciously different from what was served at other wedding feasts. My dad explained that Khaleq Babu was a Muslim and Muslims had different customs. It was years later, when I heard that he had passed away, that I recalled what a terrific storyteller he was. And I mused how my awareness of Hindu myths at an early age came from a dignified, balding Muslim gentleman who was an amazing storehouse of knowledge of Indian folklore.

The story should not be particularly surprising. Indian Islam, as scholars have noted, has long been infused with Sufi strains of thought and practice. Hindus and Muslims have lived alongside one another, mostly without violent conflict. Although intermarriage was out and inter-dining rare, the two communities engaged in routine social and commercial intercourse. Some, like Khaleq Babu, were more than commonly aware of their surrounding culture, and knew the other community's customs, rituals and myths, while most took the differences for granted.

Today, even as radical interpretations of Hinduism are stoking tension between the communities, extreme versions of Islam have come to the fore, threatening the harmony and tolerance that we Indians like to believe are inherent in our genes.

Are tolerance and liberalism ideas alien to Indian culture or are they the very essence of the idea of India? My answer is a careful 'Yes' to both questions. The ideas of liberalism and tolerance, in their modern institutionalized incarnation, can appear alien not only to Indian culture but to any traditional culture caught in the throes of change. In their present forms, these ideas were repackaged in what is broadly described as the West and developed by Western thinkers and constitutionalists over the past couple of centuries. These are ideas that emerged out of Europe's Enlightenment.

That is not to say that tolerance grew out of nothing in the minds of a few Western philosophers. Tolerance is an ancient idea, the development of which occurred over centuries in several cultures including, very importantly, India's. Today, the constitutionally enshrined idea of the democratic Republic of India rests on a foundational pillar of tolerance, without which its survival would be at stake. In the minds of millions, however, any recognition of tolerance as simply essential to India's continuance as a national entity has not yet seeped in.

Perhaps inevitably, because of sheer numbers and the course of history, much of this poor appreciation might seem to mark attitudes within the majority community alone. In fact, the reality is complex. Any discussion of intolerance and illiberalism in India today cannot remain restricted to criticism of just one community. Problems of intolerance within other communities, particularly the largest minority, will need to be discussed candidly. Intolerance is ingrained in some interpretations of Islam.

The problem of tolerance and intolerance within Islam is now a subject of worldwide debate. In the case of the brief history of the Indian republic, however, it is a subject that has so far been handled with caution, particularly by most secular politicians and intellectuals, who have tended to shy away from robust criticism of instances of intolerance when these have emerged within the Indian Muslim community.

There may be good reason for such reticence. The nations of India and Pakistan were, after all, born in calamitous bloodletting between Hindus and Muslims. Among the lives lost was that of a great apostle of tolerance, Mohandas Gandhi, killed not by a Muslim but by bullets from the gun of a Hindu nationalist, who assassinated the Father of the Nation for appearing to pander to Muslims. In the circumstances of those early years, creating an atmosphere in which all minorities left in India would feel reasonably secure was an avowed goal of the leaders of the new republic. Moreover, Pakistan had been specifically carved out to create the world's first Islamic republic; India, on the other hand, was determined to be secular and it had to be seen to be so.

As Jawaharlal Nehru said in the Constituent Assembly in April 1948:

> We have seen as a matter of fact how far communalism in politics has led us; all of us remember the grave dangers through which we have passed and the terrible consequences

> we have seen. In any event, now there is no alternative; and we must have it clearly in our minds and in the mind of the country that the alliance of religion and politics in the shape of communalism is a most dangerous alliance, and it yields the most abnormal kind of illegitimate brood.

Secularism was, therefore, India's clear choice. Interestingly, in the same speech, Nehru warned:

> ... the combination of politics and of religion in the narrowest sense of the word, resulting in communal politics is... a most dangerous combination and must be put an end to... It is harmful to the majority, but probably most harmful to any minority that seeks to have some advantage from it. I think even the past history of India will show that. But in any event a minority in an independent state which seeks to isolate itself does some injury to the cause of the country, and most of all it injures its own interests, because inevitably it puts a barrier between itself and the others, a barrier not on the religious plane but on the political plane – sometimes even to some extent on the economic plane; and it can never really exercise the influence which it legitimately ought to aspire to exercise if it functions in that way.

That was two years before the republic was born. During the six decades since then, the nation has been unable to rid itself of religion-driven politics. In many instances, political groups representing the majority community of Hindus have taken provocative positions against minority identity issues, as I have already noted. In others, the leaderships of minority communities have taken positions inconsistent with the functioning of a secular state that regards itself as a liberal democracy.

Take the case of personal laws. When the Constitution of India came into effect on 26 January 1950, Article 44 read: 'The State shall endeavour to secure for the citizens of India a uniform civil code throughout the territory of India.' The endeavour continues. To this day, a uniform civil code hasn't come about.

The reform of personal laws was a bone of contention in the Constituent Assembly. For Nehru and B.R. Ambedkar, who was the chairman of the drafting committee as well as law minister, a common civil code for all citizens was a defining feature of any secular democracy. Several members of the assembly, Muslim as well as Hindu, thought otherwise. Muslim members argued that the British had not interfered with personal laws, so the new Indian state should not do so either. They said that Muslim laws of marriage, divorce and inheritance were dependent on religion; that it was too early to meddle with personal laws; and that a uniform civil code would violate a constitutional provision, which was the freedom to practise one's religion.

Ambedkar tried to refute such arguments by insisting that if personal laws were to be kept unaffected India would be unable to carry out social reform. Nonetheless, introducing a secular constitution or encouraging a secular frame of mind in a deeply religious country was not going to be easy. Nehru and Ambedkar had a fight on their hands.

They soon realized that while there was a sizeable section among Hindus who would be behind progressive legislation, among Muslims the liberal element did not have critical mass. Before long, after bruising battles within and outside Parliament, they gave up the idea of legislating a comprehensive uniform civil code but pursued the idea of a Hindu code bill which eventually passed into law as the Hindu Marriage Act of 1955 and the Hindu Succession, Minority and Guardianship, and Adoptions and Maintenance Acts of 1956. Muslim personal law was left unaffected by progressive legislation, to the relief of Muslim leaders, who profusely thanked the government.

The fact that Muslims were the largest minority in a secular nation, and therefore deserving of a degree of special consideration, seems to have played a role in influencing both Nehru and Ambedkar. India was, after all, the non-Pakistan and its new leaders were ready to go to a considerable length to demonstrate that Muslims could live without discrimination in secular India, as in fact several million had chosen to do by opting not to migrate to Pakistan after Partition. As Ambedkar himself acknowledged, the government would be 'foolish... not to realize the sentiments of different communities in this country'. Not everyone agreed with that view.

A Hindu Mahasabha leader, N.C. Chatterjee, asked in Parliament why in a secular state the same law should not apply to all communities. If the government believed, for instance, that monogamy was good and polygamy bad, 'then why not rescue our Muslim sisters from that curse and that plight?' he wondered. Even the socialist J.B. Kripalani thought the law was unfair and the government was being hypocritical. 'You must bring it also for the Muslim community. Take it from me that the Muslim community is prepared to have it but you are not brave enough to do it,' he said.

Asked in Parliament why he had not introduced a uniform civil code for all citizens, Nehru replied that such a code indeed had his 'extreme sympathy' but he did not think 'at the present moment the time is ripe in India for me to try to push it through. I want to prepare the ground for it.' Sixty years after the republic came into being, the time is still not ripe and the ground is not ready for a uniform civil code. Given the state of India's political leadership, it is probably too late now for this to happen.

We can thus assert that secularism in India became a doctrine that was unevenly applied across the religious spectrum. That might be akin to taking a purist and, in the Indian context, impractical view of secularism. More of that argument later.

As Nehru and Ambedkar, both avowed secularists, realized in the early days of the republic, secularism had to become an attitude of inclusive tolerance towards all religious groups within the confines of India and not a doctrine of any strict separation of religion from public life or an attempt to keep the government deliberately neutral in matters religious.

The very nature of the Indian Union came in the way of a more rigid application of secular principles. As I noted earlier, making a nation out of the diverse economically backward and poorly educated people who lived in the subcontinent, and that under a democratic constitution, was a unique enterprise in history. In order to accommodate the myriad aspirations as well as anxieties of each group, linguistic, caste and religious, India's leaders had to be prudent as well as flexible to the degree possible. Any neutral application of a universal civil code for all communities was politically very difficult in practice.

The consequence was, however, that Hindu nationalists gained a point to support their contention that Congress leaders were hypocritical secularists. Throughout the six decades of India's existence as a republic, they have repeatedly chastized 'pseudo-secularists', who they feel are only too willing to bend over backwards to appease Muslims but are far less inclined to accommodate the religious demands of Hindus.

That is, of course, quite untrue because the Indian state today appears ready to bend over backwards to demands, many of them outlandish, of almost every religious group. Just count the number of official state or national holidays in the Indian calendar in respect of religious leaders or auspicious days of every significant religious community – Hindu, Sikh, Muslim, Christian, Jain, Buddhist and Parsi – and you will not find any other nation, and a secular one at that, which downs its shutters as frequently as India does for religious reasons. Alternatively, consider the way local religious cults and communities merrily usurp chunks of public property, including public thoroughfares, to erect temples, shrines and mosques but are rarely, if ever, forced to remove them. On the contrary, at some places such shrines have become major religious centres visited regularly by the masses as well as politicians, officials and movie stars. The state simply stands aside respectfully.

Nevertheless, the case of Muslims in India is exceptional for two reasons. One is the sheer size and consequent political significance of India's Muslim community. It is undoubtedly the largest such minority of Muslims anywhere and it has a voice in several constituencies of the country in determining electoral outcomes. At the time of Partition, the number of Muslims living in the Indian subcontinent was the largest of any Islamic community in the world. Today, India's Muslim minority population is the largest among Muslim societies anywhere outside Indonesia and Pakistan. This community as a whole has to be seen as having exercised a choice by continuing to live in India rather than moving to Pakistan. The implicit assumption behind the choice was that Muslims, along with adherents of other faiths, would be able to practise their religion freely as guaranteed by India's secular constitution.

How free would that be? Would the state permit specific Islamic laws or practices to trump secular laws of the land applicable in theory to all citizens? Should the state make special allowances for Muslims in deference to their religion?

Matters came to a head in 1985, when the Supreme Court passed a judgment in favour of Shah Bano, a Muslim divorcee, by ruling that her erstwhile husband should pay her alimony. Muslim politicians and religious leaders went into a frenzy, calling the ruling an attack on Islamic law and the Muslim way of life. Widespread agitations led the Congress government of Rajiv Gandhi in 1986 to effectively bypass the court judgment by passing a Muslim Women's (Protection of Rights on Divorce) Bill, which made it no longer possible for Muslim women to follow Shah Bano's lead. Whereas the Supreme Court had upheld secular law, the government of the day felt compelled by political circumstance to make a special case for Muslim citizens.

A second reason why Muslims, or rather radical Islamic ideologues, seem to want exceptional treatment is an apparent conflict, inherent in certain versions of Islam, between nationalism and global pan-Islamism. In this view, any true Muslim should let allegiance to the Islamic ummah override primary loyalty to a particular nation.

This, of course, is not a problem unique to India. The world is wrestling with it. When Major Nidal Malik Hasan went on the rampage in Fort Hood, Texas, in late 2009, killing thirteen American soldiers, he apparently did it because he did not want to fight other Muslims anywhere in the world even though he had sworn allegiance to the American flag when he had signed up for the US military. He responded to a call of the ummah, allegedly goaded through the Internet by a radical cleric in Yemen.

To the best of my knowledge, no Indian soldier has agonized over such a dilemma. India has fought several wars during its six decades of existence and most of those wars have been against an Islamic nation. Muslim soldiers have fought bravely for the Indian armed forces and some have been decorated for their skill and bravery. Indian Muslims are overwhelmingly Indians first. They see themselves as citizens who happen to be Muslim, much like their fellow citizens who might be Hindu or Christian or Sikh or atheist. There is, however, a radical fringe that thinks otherwise and sections of India's political and clerical Muslim leadership opportunistically pander to the fundamentalists who see the Islamic ummah in a state of siege. An example of such opportunism is the Salman Rushdie affair, which I shall presently discuss.

Indian Islam has for centuries had a distinct Sufi strain running through it. Islam initially came to India with Arab traders and the earliest Islamic communities were in the coastal regions. Later, Muslims of Turkish origin from Central Asia brought Islam to north India. The expansion of Islam in the subcontinent was through both trade and conquest but Sufi preachers and pirs played a crucial role in that spread.

Scholars of Islam have written extensively about how that expansion happened. For my purposes, I can note that right up to the nineteenth century, the essence of Indian Islam was based more on a Sufi advocacy of devotional intensity and mystical love than on any overwhelming concern about the fate or tribulations of a larger Islamic ummah. While the ulema were experts on the laws of the sharia, Sufi saints and preachers were specialists in meditative skills. That is not to say that Sufis were somehow disconnected from the politics of the palace. Sufism in India has always been entwined with social trends and political intrigues of the state, especially during the reign of the Mughal emperors from 1526 to 1858, when Sufis gave moral legitimacy to the monarchs and in turn enjoyed enormous influence in the emperors' courts.

The situation began to change in the nineteenth century. Two trends were probably responsible for the change. One was the growth of 'reform' movements, often through Arab Wahhabi influence, in parts of the Islamic world, including

India. The second was a British imperial preference to see Indian subjects in categories of communities like Muslim and Hindu and Sikh, which consolidated group identities. Because the growing awareness of a Muslim group identity happened in the context of a minority trying to define itself separately from a Hindu majority, the reformist effort to redefine Islam was also an attempt to assert boundaries between the two communities. Consequently, Sufism came under attack from the reformists because that strain of Islam did not distinguish itself in stark terms from the local culture.

By the second half of the nineteenth century, a number of Muslim thinkers became convinced, influenced to an extent by modernizing efforts already under way in the Hindu community, that the adoption of European values, like the rule of law and the pursuit of science, would be an effective way to revitalize the Muslims of India. The standard bearer of these 'modernists' was Sir Sayid Ahmed Khan. He founded the Aligarh School in 1877 with the objective of modernizing Islam through European education. Students of Aligarh were urged to distance themselves from any blind adherence to Islamic doctrine, to modernize the sharia, and to unshackle their minds from the rigidities taught by the ulema. The modernists even demanded that the sharia be withdrawn from the civil sphere. Inevitably, the ulema became hostile.

Even as the modernists tried to create a new identity for Muslims, the ulema and other conservatives reinvigorated efforts to galvanize the masses towards an identity defined in Islamic terms. Maulana Maududi, an Islamic scholar, rose to prominence in the early twentieth century by asserting that the 'law of Allah should become the law by which people lead their lives'. In other words, there should be no separation of religious and civil life, contrary to what the modernists were saying.

Maududi founded the Jamaat-i-Islami in 1941. Although his ideas influenced a growing demand for the creation of Pakistan, Maududi himself rejected the ideology of nationalism, which he described as a Western conspiracy to subjugate Muslims. Importantly, he argued that Muslims should follow Islamic universalism. Thus it was through the influence of intellectual leaders like Maududi that the notion of ummah gained the upper hand over nationalism in the minds of many Indian Muslims.

The global fire that raged following the publication of Salman Rushdie's *The Satanic Verses* began from a spark lighted in India. Rushdie is a Mumbai-born British author, who impressed the world in the 1970s and 1980s with a series of novels written in a style known as magic realism. He had been born to Indian Muslim parents but was not a practising Muslim by the time he emerged as a writer of serious worth.

The Satanic Verses was published in Britain in September 1988. The story goes that in a review of the book published in an Indian daily, the reviewer had speculated on a few passages that could be construed by Islamic hardliners as blasphemous. Some opportunistic leaders of the Muslim community picked up the strand. They began mobilizing mass demonstrations, egged on by the Opposition Janata Party, demanding a ban on the book by the government. Within days, the Congress government of Rajiv Gandhi caved in to the demand. The rest is now history.

Banning books is not uncommon in India. It is not even unconstitutional. Article 19, which promises freedom of expression, has a sub-clause (2) which sets out all kinds of conditions under which the government, meaning politicians and bureaucrats, might curb that freedom. That any book that offends anyone's sensibilities, including incendiary religious texts, need not be read or bought or picked up at the library, is not an argument that bureaucrats or politicians favour. They would rather demonstrate their power to protect citizens by banning the book.

In the case of Salman Rushdie's *The Satanic Verses*, the Indian ban began a process that, in my reckoning, can be seen as a turning point in modern history. As events snowballed into a worldwide controversy, the extreme Islamic cry to save an embattled ummah became a truly global phenomenon for the first time. Furious waves of Islamism began to wash up on distant shores, as a perceived threat to the ummah became the rallying call for radical Muslim ideologues across the world.

An excellent account, by Andrew Anthony, of the events that followed India's banning of the book came out in the British newspaper, *The Observer*, on 11 January 2009, the twentieth anniversary of Ayatollah Khomeini's fatwa imposing a death sentence on Rushdie. For our purpose, the unfolding of events is important to recall.

On the heels of the success of Indian Muslim leaders to get the book banned in India, writes Anthony, some men of Indian origin, who worked for the Saudi-funded Islamic Foundation of Leicester, suggested a campaign to have the book banned in the UK. The Jamaat-i-Islami, the party founded by Maulana Maududi, which had a significant political profile in Pakistan, organized the campaign. It was, however, a Saudi body, the United Kingdom Action Committee on Islamic Affairs, which built up pressure in Britain against the book. Saudi clerics began planning a trial of Rushdie in absentia.

Iran had not yet banned the book. Noticing the protests in India and the UK, a group of clerics from the holy city of Qom read out a section of the book to Ayatollah Khomeini, 'including the part featuring a mad imam in exile, which was an obvious caricature of Khomeini', writes Anthony. Thereupon the ayatollah delivered his infamous fatwa.

The affair was as much a starting point for the globalization of radical Islam as it was a jockeying for influence in the Muslim world between Iran and Saudi Arabia. The Sunni Saudis had for years been exporting their version of a fundamentalist, or Salafi, brand of Islam; Shia Iran, after a humiliating war against Saddam Hussein's Iraq, was itching to re-establish its credentials as leader of the Islamic revolution. The uproar in South Asia and Britain over Rushdie's book provided Iran the opportunity.

On the day the fatwa was issued, Rushdie went into hiding. He moved in with a British Special Branch protection team to the Lygon Arms Hotel in the Cotswolds. That same evening Channel 4 carried a pre-recorded interview with the author. 'It's very simple in this country,' said Rushdie when he was asked about a growing demand that his book be withdrawn from stores. 'If you don't want to read a book, you don't have to read it. It's very hard to be offended by *The Satanic Verses*; it requires a long period of intense reading. It's a quarter of a million words.'

For a decade after Khomeini's fatwa was issued urging Muslims to kill him, Rushdie led a besieged life. He had bodyguards around him twenty-four hours a day and had to move from one hiding spot to another every time the security forces became aware of various plots to assassinate him. His marriage to Marianne Wiggins, an American writer, could not take the pressure and broke up. Politicians did not want to be seen in public with him. British Airways declined to fly him for fear of endangering their staff. He could not go to the Indian subcontinent and had a hard time trying to travel anywhere. Once, when he did manage to fly out of Britain incognito, he stayed in Washington DC with a friend, the writer Christopher Hitchens. 'When he was staying at my house at Thanksgiving of 1993, so were about a dozen heavily armed members of the United States' finest anti-terrorist forces,' Hitchens later told Anthony of *The Observer*. All this for a man who was just a writer, and that too of a dense book which perhaps none of those radicals out for his blood had read.

Meanwhile, demonstrations by Muslims continued in the subcontinent. On 24 February 1989, a dozen people were killed and forty wounded when the police opened fire on Muslims rioting in Mumbai against *The Satanic Verses*. In Pakistan, six persons were killed and eighty-three wounded when the police opened fire outside a US information centre in Islamabad on demonstrators who demanded the banning of the book in America.

Twenty years later, the fatwa has not been withdrawn. Rushdie, now a resident of New York, is a relatively free person who can move around, write and speak. Sporadically, however, the embers of rage against him burst out in small flames. In January 2008, for example, when the family of Adi Godrej, a major industrialist in Mumbai, hosted the author on a brief holiday in the city where he was born, the All India Ulema Council fumed that the family had not cared for the sentiments of Muslims.

'We really hope Mr Godrej realizes the hurt he has caused us and says sorry for it,' said Maulana Mehmood Daryabadi, a council official. 'Otherwise, we are asking Muslims all over to boycott his company's products.'

The Maulana did not bother to explain why the Zoroastrian Godrej family should be obliged to think about hurting Muslim sentiments, or heed a murderous foreign fatwa from two decades ago, when inviting a guest home. The assumption is that *all* communities, in India or anywhere else, must care for specific Islamic grievances, global and local, or be ready to face consequences, which could well be dire.

An unduly nervous government finally granted Rushdie a visa in 1999, and in April 2000, he visited India for the first time since the fatwa was issued. His visit happened in the glare of TV cameras and reporters wherever he went. Speaking to the press in Mumbai, he said: 'I have to leave the past behind to be able to go on.'

The past, however, still haunts India, if not Rushdie. Like Rushdie, others who live by their creative abilities have had to face the wrath of those who refuse to tolerate any difference of opinion or cultural diversity in this land of unbounded variety. The fury of the intolerant Indian casts a long shadow over India.

Six

SENSE AND SENSITIVITY

In 1996, an art critic, Dyaneshwar Nadkarni, published a book on the works of Maqbool Fida Husain, widely regarded as modern India's greatest artist. A drawing in the book started a tsunami of intolerance, thanks to which Husain eventually had to escape the country and take refuge in a Gulf nation.

The book included a line drawing of the Hindu goddess Saraswati, which, in a stylized way, showed her in the nude. This was nothing unusual. Several artists through the ages have drawn goddesses in the nude. Nude art was hardly unknown in India, as the ancient temple art of Khajuraho and Konarak amply testify.

Husain himself had drawn a number of goddesses and mythological figures in the nude over the years. This drawing of a faceless and nude Saraswati was over two decades old. However, a Hindu nationalist magazine in Madhya Pradesh reproduced the picture from Nadkarni's book and called it a blasphemous act by a Muslim artist.

Frenzy built up in Hindutva circles, fanned by activists of the Bajrang Dal. They set fire to some of Husain's paintings in Ahmedabad. A national campaign against the artist spread far and wide and a couple of his other drawings, one of the goddess Durga and the other a stylized map of India, came under fire. The drawing of Durga, like that of Saraswati, was abstractly nude; the map of India was in the shape of a female nude with one breast pointing towards the Arabian Sea. Confused and distraught, Husain apologized to those whom he might have inadvertently hurt.

The agitations petered out after a few days, but the matter did not die. In April 1998, a gallery in New Delhi displayed a lithograph by Husain, which the artist had named 'Sita Rescued.' The work, which depicted a scene from the Ramayana showing Hanuman rescuing Sita sitting on his tail, had been exhibited earlier in the respected Bharat Bhavan in Bhopal and, as several critics pointed out, could be seen as erotic or insulting by only those who were determined to do so. However, an artist, who had a personal grouse against the gallery, took the picture to the Vishwa Hindu Parishad.

The VHP stormed the Delhi gallery. Then, pictures of the lithograph appeared in the press, along with news of the raid. Hindu extremists in Mumbai entered the fray. On 1 May, which happened to be Maharashtra Day, Bajrang Dal activists forced their way into the Cuffe Parade home of Husain in south Mumbai and ransacked it. Husain was not home at the time; out of fear, he did not return to the apartment until 4 May.

Husain offered to 'face an agnipariksha', or test by fire, as he put it. He suggested the setting up of a committee of three, an art critic, a lawyer, and a representative of the Vishwa Hindu Parishad, to sift through his entire collection of works. He would be ready to destroy any drawing that the committee found objectionable.

In an earlier interview to the news magazine *Frontline*, he had said: 'I believe in my country, and I am a painter. I only know the seven colours.' In striking contrast to the artist's conciliatory tone, the chief of Mumbai's regional party, the Shiv Sena, raved in support of the raid on his house. 'If Husain can conduct himself as he pleases with regard to our gods and goddesses, we won't be averse to entering his house,' fumed Bal Thackeray. He added: 'If Husain can step into Hindustan, what is wrong if we enter his house.' It seemed that in Thackeray's eyes, Husain was a foreigner in India.

And that's what he de facto became. To cut a long story short, in the wake of persistent hostility and legal persecution, the artist decided to leave India and settle in the United Arab Emirates. Hindu organizations filed hundreds of court cases against him under British-era sections of the Indian Penal Code, which allow prosecution of anyone for hurting the feelings of a class by insulting a religion or religious beliefs. In September 2009, the Supreme Court gave him a reprieve by dismissing one of the many cases. However, with other cases pending and the likelihood of one of the many physical threats being carried out if he returned, Husain has become an exile.

Not just Hindu extremists, even some Muslim groups have given him a hard time. His film *Meenaxi: A Tale of Three Cities* had to be withdrawn in 2009 from theatres following protests by the All India Ulema Council, the Jamaat-i-Islami, the All India Muslim Council, and other groups. They objected to a song that they felt was blasphemous. They approached the police commissioner of Mumbai to have the film banned; Husain responded by withdrawing the film.

In 2006, the ninety-year-old Husain had an exhibition of his paintings in London. Inaugurating the show, the Indian high commissioner, Kamlesh Sharma, said: 'Husain's career and success mirrors closely the meteoric rise of contemporary Indian art on the international stage.' Yet the exhibition had to be shut down following threats from Hindu nationalists. In India, art exhibitions no longer risk showing his works.

Husain, who was offered citizenship by the government of Qatar, accepted it in March 2010 and turned in his passport to the Indian embassy in Dubai, where he now lives. Such is the fate of an iconic citizen of secular, democratic India.

Artists, writers, dramatists and film-makers have become easy targets of Hindu and Muslim extremists in India. Husain's is the most prominent example. Other artists have had to face the intolerant and often violent fury of religious bigots. Even those who are studying art are not spared, as a 2009 incident in Vadodara demonstrated.

S. Chandramohan, a final year student artist at the highly reputed Maharaja Sayajirao University of Baroda, participated in a students' art exhibition at the Faculty of Fine Arts on the university campus. His works included a drawing of Durga, in a birthing position, giving birth to rakshasas or demons. The exhibition was not open to the public. That did not stop a bunch of VHP activists from storming into the exhibition and beating up Chandramohan on the ground that he had offended religious sentiments.

To the astonishment of students and professors present at the event, the police, who had followed the extremists into the exhibition hall, arrested Chandramohan. When the acting dean of the Faculty of Fine Arts, Shivaji Panikkar, tried to intervene, the police threatened to arrest him as well. Following a nationwide uproar over the artist's arrest, the police released Chandramohan on bail after a few days.

Interestingly, a few Christian priests joined the local leader of the VHP, Niraj Jain, to demand apologies from Chandramohan and Panikkar. One of the allegedly offensive paintings showed a cross floating above a bathroom commode; this gave the priests an opportunity to display their grievance even though Hindu extremists had in recent years attacked several Christian missionaries across the state of Gujarat.

The vice chancellor of the university, Manoj Soni, declined to file a police case against the intruders or to extend support to Chandramohan. To the dismay of students and faculty, he met Niraj Jain and later asked Chandramohan and Panikkar to apologize for offending religious sentiments, even though the exhibition was not open to the public and was, in fact, a part of the fine arts examination procedure.

To those who are aware of the depiction of erotic art in temple sculpture all over India, the outrage of the orthodox at nudity in modern art can be baffling. Indian temples and shrines have traditionally depicted images of dancers, musicians and romantic couples. From the tenth century or thereabouts, say art historians, erotic themes surfaced in temple sculpture; sensuality and outright sexual acts were displayed in places of worship. Erotic desire was not seen as alien to spirituality. Jayadeva's *Gita Govinda* is an example of this.

'In that period of Indian history tantric ideas on the compatibility of human sexuality with human spirituality entered the mainstream,' writes art critic Madanjeet Singh in *The Hindu* of 18 May 2007. The most intimate and personal of human interactions, he added, were now sculpted in stone, 'decrying fundamentalism and demonstrating that Indian religion and morality were based not on worldly denial but instead on an unabashed acceptance of essential human urges.'

There seem to be two contrasting and fiercely contested views of the idea of India today.

A letter circulating on the web after Husain took up Qatari citizenship angrily presents one of those views. It is addressed to N. Ram, editor of *The Hindu,* and is harshly critical of the stand taken by the paper in urging Husain's return to India. Interestingly, it is not written by a Hindu fanatic; the writer is a Christian woman, Hilda Raja, who once taught at a Chennai college and now lives in Vadodara. She argues her case well.

First, she says, Husain has become a citizen of Qatar, which is not known to respect freedom of expression or democracy. She challenges the artist living there to paint a picture of Mohammed, one that is fully clothed unlike his nude portrayals of Hindu goddesses. She asks why no one protested in India when Salman Rushdie's book, *The Satanic Verses*, was banned or why Taslima Nasrin continues to be 'hunted and hounded'. Don't they deserve freedom of expression? Why does the media not condemn Islamic intolerance but is ever ready to blame the Sangh parivar?

Next, she wonders why Husain's artistic freedom 'seems to run unfettered in an expression of sexual perversion only when he envisages Hindu gods and goddesses'. It is Husain's business to enjoy 'painting his sexual perversion', she allows, 'But why use Saraswati and Sita for his perverted expressions?' She goes on to note that Husain painted Indira Gandhi during the Emergency in the 1970s as Durga and had supported the suspension of freedom for artists and writers. It seems to her that 'elite secularists' and the media use a soft secularism to judge Muslim wrongdoings.

Now the point about Qatar is a smart one but quite irrelevant. Those of us feeling just as infuriated as Hilda Raja, from a diametrically opposing angle, about Husain's inability to return to India, are not exactly engaged in a debate about the quality of freedom in Qatar. Frankly, we don't care. We are angry at the inability of our own democratic culture to protect the right of an artist to express himself in any way he likes. Yes, many of us did protest the ban on Rushdie and have taken clear stands against the harassment of Taslima.

Second, what is so 'perverted' about Husain's drawing mythological figures in the nude? Renowned critics in India and abroad have almost unanimously come out in support of Husain's depictions of Saraswati and Durga as fine examples of artistic imagination. Why should we – those of us who feel frustrated at the Indian state's repeated caving in to the whims of religious fanatics – accept any definition of perversion by persons who may have an uninformed understanding of liberty or suffer far too much from a sexually repressive culture to recognize real perversion?

Here's a fundamental issue: In a genuine democracy, it is perversion to demand that your viewpoint be accepted to the exclusion of all others. You, as a religiously sensitive individual, have every right to protest, write letters to the editor, stage demonstrations, cry yourself hoarse against nudity in art, but you have no right to force my voice to be silent or make it impossible for me to write or paint at will. If you don't like what I write or draw, the solution is easy. Simply don't read or see it.

That raises the ever so delicate matter of religious sensitivity. In a secular democracy, those of us who are non-religious but sensitive need space to express ourselves. The Indian Constitution officially gives us that space; unfortunately, going by the weak-kneed responses of various governments, state and Central, the feelings of the religiously minded invariably trump our secular sensitivities. We feel enraged that despite our constitutionally sanctioned freedoms we always have to stand down to those who might be hurt on one religious ground or the other.

Some of us would like to shout from the rooftop: A pox on all houses of organized religion! They have brought much misery, death and destruction to humanity. That's about it; we would just like to shout or write or paint or demonstrate. We don't want to force anyone to our viewpoint by ransacking galleries or burning works of art or physically threatening those who disagree with us, Hindu or Muslim.

Controversies over artistic expression take place in all democracies. That is why they are called democracies. In the United States, for example, many Christian groups were upset about Martin Scorsese's movie *The Last Temptation of Christ.* They demonstrated, peacefully, outside several theatres in the country. Those who wanted to see the movie could go in and watch it. All the state authorities did was to provide police protection at theatres, both for demonstrators and movie viewers.

When an artist of the calibre of Husain renounces his citizenship of India, some of us proud Indians are entitled to weep because we too can be sensitive. But we would fight to defend the right to freedom of expression of those who mock our tears.

Artists are not the only victims of zealots acting as guardians of public morality. Movie theatres have been attacked for showing films that were not to the liking of one fanatical group or the other, such as when hooligans attacked cinema halls for showing Deepa Mehta's *Fire*, which included scenes depicting a vaguely lesbian relationship.

Towards the end of 2009, the Shiv Sena in Mumbai took on Shah Rukh Khan, India's most popular movie star, and tried to stop the screening of his film *My Name Is Khan*. Their complaint was that Khan had criticized the manner in which a recent auction of cricketers for the Indian Premier League had excluded Pakistani players. The Sena, however, had taken on too much, as its leaders realized. The man was too big a national icon for any regional outfit. They backed off when Khan refused to apologize and drew on his national mass appeal to stand up to the Sena.

Around 14 February every year, goons raid shops selling Valentine's Day cards. Such romantic behaviour is not part of Indian culture, they say, as they threaten shopkeepers and trawl parks to pounce on young couples who might be snuggling too close for Indian cultural comfort as defined by these self-appointed moral guardians. They clearly believe that such threats of violent consequences and destruction of property are an intrinsic part of some honourable Indian tradition.

In January 2009, a bunch of Sri Ram Sene activists roughed up a group of young men and women in a pub in Mangalore, Karnataka. Television cameras captured images of the Sene men beating up women to teach them a lesson in morality. The founder of the group, P. Muthalik, said he had no regrets because his men were protecting people from immoral activities, such as what he termed 'obscene dancing'.

The Sene activists were later arrested. The state inspector general of police, A.M. Prasad, said: 'Nobody has the right to take law into their own hands.' Curiously, the state minister in charge of the district, Krishna Palemar, said that pubs would not be allowed to stay open beyond 11 pm, which was a reasonable call, but added that 'obscene dance will not be allowed in our district', which was the Ram Sene's line.

The Sene had firm views on what women should and should not do. Pravin Valke, a founding member of the Sri Ram Sene in Mangalore, told the *Indian Express* on 3 February 2009:

> These girls [who go to pubs] come from all over India; [they] drink, smoke, and walk around in the night spoiling the traditional girls of Mangalore. Why should girls go to pubs? Are they going to serve their future husbands alcohol? Should they not learn to make chapatis? Bars and pubs should be for men only. We wanted to ensure that all women in Mangalore are home by 7 pm.

Karnataka is a state of which Bengaluru, globalization's symbolic city, is the state capital. But it is also a state that has recorded the second highest number of attacks, after Orissa, against Christians. In 2008, the state had at least 112 anti-Christian attacks by Hindu extremists spread across twenty-nine districts, according to the Global Council of Indian Christians. Anti-Christian violence in Orissa was, however, worse. In September 2008, 127 people were killed and Hindu fanatics destroyed 315 villages, over 4,500 houses, 250 churches and thirteen schools in Orissa.

When it comes to parochial intolerance though, Maharashtra leads the pack.

Mumbai, the capital city of Maharashtra, has long prided itself on being the financial capital of India. It has also maintained a cosmopolitan character in a way that perhaps no other city in India can rival. Today, however, it is becoming increasingly known for intolerance, nurtured principally by the Shiv Sena and its offshoot, the Maharashtra Navnirman Sena.

Bal Thackeray, the Shiv Sena's founder, first drew attention in the 1960s when he launched a parochial campaign against south Indians living and working in Mumbai. The campaign struck a chord among some Maharashtrians, especially the young and the jobless. The Shiv Sena gradually became a regional force to reckon with in Mumbai and its surroundings. Although it didn't catch significant wind with most Maharashtrians elsewhere in the state, it became influential in pockets. By the time it shared state governmental power with the BJP in the mid-1990s, the Shiv Sena's principal rabble-rousing cry was no longer against south Indians; it was against Muslims. Strong Maharashtrian identity politics remained the mainstay of its platform but it found communal politics also paying.

The party's fortunes began to decline in the early years of the new century. It still remained a force in Maharashtrian politics but, with an aging leader and infighting in the party, its appeal began to lose some shine. In 2004, it and its then partner, the BJP, lost the state elections to a Congress-Nationalist Congress Party combine, but the relatively close electoral outcome suggested that the Sena remained a significant player. It was the continuing infighting, chiefly a struggle for succession between Bal Thackeray's son, Uddhav, and his nephew, Raj, that weakened the Shiv Sena's hold.

When Uddhav became his father's anointed successor, Raj realized his future in the party would have to be as second fiddle. In December 2005, he quit.

Raj Thackeray founded the Maharashtra Navnirman Sena in March 2006. Uddhav and he struggled to gain the upper hand in attracting support from the Shiv Sena's followers. In his first foray into electoral battle, the municipal election of 2007, the MNS fared poorly. However, in early 2008, Raj found an opportunity to revive his uncle's line against outsiders in Mumbai. While the uncle's grouse had been against south Indians, Raj decided to go after north Indians.

In January 2008, two women were molested in the northern suburb of Juhu. One of the alleged molesters was a Maharshtrian man. Raj came out in vigorous defence of the man, saying that outsiders were to blame for the attack. Thus began his violent crusade against north Indians, in the main poor migrants from Bihar and Uttar Pradesh.

The 2009 state assembly elections showed that the MNS had made inroads into the Shiv Sena's territory in Mumbai, Pune and Nashik. Although by splitting the Sena support he helped the Congress-NCP combine retain power, Raj Thackeray had captured a huge chunk of the Shiv Sena's base. His party's performance also demonstrated that despite the decline of the Shiv Sena, its sons-of-the-soil slogan could still attract support. Today, the two Senas continue a parochial contest for the Maharashtrian mind though the chances of their success remain more or less restricted to Greater Mumbai and Pune. An anti-outsider campaign resonates less in other areas because migrants from other states tend to move to industrial and commercial hubs.

The campaign has embarrassed even the BJP and the RSS. The leader of the BJP, L.K. Advani, spoke out against such divisive politics: 'No political party should say or do anything that weakens the country's unity or undermines the Constitution.' However, groups like the Shiv Sena and the MNS are less concerned about the stability of the country than about widening their narrow local support bases. The problem is that if such fringe groups can successfully spread their cancerous hatred in various parts of the country, they can effectively attack the foundations of this secular republic.

To an extent the seeds of regional parochialism lie in Nehruvian India's decision to opt for linguistic states. Each province is effectively a sub-nation, with its own distinctive language and cultural habits tied to the language. For the most part, however, linguistic sub-nations have recognized the unique nature of the Indian experiment and have gone along with the national aspiration of sustaining unity with diversity. Supporting that goal means allowing the free movement of people across state borders. If all states stopped such movement in narrow self-interest, the Indian nation would cease to exist and a great venture in nation building would be at an end.

India is an exceptional experiment that has outlasted other ambitious attempts to create one nation out of many. India's founding fathers wisely opted to create a republic because they knew that no monarch could hold such a nation together in this day and age. Similarly, democracy for the new republic was not just an option; it was the only viable choice. This extent of diversity demanded institutionalized outlets for the competing wisps of steam that would inevitably build up while we attempted to build a national consensus in matters of public policy and opinion. No wonder far-sighted thinkers like Gandhi and Tagore plugged 'unity in diversity' as a bond for the nation-in-the-making throughout the struggle for independence. Diversity was the reality; unity was a work-in-progress for which the founding fathers laid the groundwork.

Violent moral policing was not common in the early decades of the republic. It has gathered frequency over the past couple of decades, possibly as a result of competitive moral posturing for political territory by various groups. Much of the policing centres on an apparent need of such groups to keep women in their place.

Taslima Nasrin fled her home country Bangladesh after Islamic extremists sought her death when her book *Lajja* (*Shame*), about violence by Muslims against Hindus in her country, was published in 1994. Nasrin, born into a Muslim family, is a secular humanist and criticizes religion as an exploitative and oppressive force.

She initially took shelter in Kolkata. Unfortunately, the authorities in India were not only unable to provide her security for long, but taking a cue from the Islamic Republic of Bangladesh, they themselves banned a few of her books (*Lajja* and *Dwikhondito*), as they were afraid of upsetting Muslims in West Bengal. She has had to endure repeated harassment in India from Muslim clerics and radicals, and has often had to migrate to European countries for temporary shelter before homing back to India every now and again. Her writings, which have won freedom awards in the West, have enraged Islamic radicals in India, where she has received grudging shelter from governments in New Delhi and Kolkata but not the support she might have expected from a secular nation.

In a cynical compromise of ideological purity, the secular Communist Party of India (Marxist) in power in West Bengal in 2003 banned her book, the autobiographical *Dwikhondito*, in which she had criticized Islamic societies for degrading women under the guise of religion. After opportunistic Muslim politicians sparked protests that led to riots, which had to be quelled by the armed forces, the CPI(M) had clearly become afraid of losing Muslim votes in the state. The Calcutta High Court, to its credit, heard an appeal against the ban and, in 2005, declared it 'untenable' before setting it aside. *Dwikhondito* reappeared in bookshops, but Taslima Nasrin remained a hunted woman. She moved from city to city and hideout to hideout, running for her life.

In August 2007, the Hyderabad Press Club held a book launch to release a Telugu translation of one of her novels. Muslim radicals attacked her at the conference. Several men threw objects at her while some shouted for her death. With a bruised forehead, she managed to leave the venue escorted by the police, who later arrested some of the rowdies and their instigators, including three state legislators.

Taslima Nasrin is still on the run, from her home in Bangladesh as well as from West Bengal, Andhra Pradesh, Karnataka, and, it seems, from wherever Muslim extremists find it convenient to use her as a scapegoat to whip up mob fury. Their grievance: How dare this mere woman, born a Muslim, criticize Islam and speak her mind!

Occasionally, strident Muslim moralizing in India strays into the ludicrous. Sania Mirza of Hyderabad is the country's best female tennis player. Although her world ranking has slipped lately, she has broken a couple of times into the list of top thirty women players of the world. Mullahs, however, don't like what she wears on court.

In 2005, soon after she had played in the fourth round of the US Open tournament, losing to then world number one Maria Sharapova, her nationwide popularity and high profile caught the attention of some Muslim clerics. Haseeb-ul-Hasan Siddiqui, a cleric with the Sunni Ulema Board, led a group of mullahs to issue a fatwa demanding that she cover herself up on court instead of wearing short skirts and tee shirts, which they ruled were 'un-Islamic' and 'corrupting'. Said Siddiqui: 'The dress she wears on tennis courts not only doesn't cover large parts of her body but leaves nothing to the imagination.' Responded Sania: 'As long as I am winning, people shouldn't care whether my skirt is six inches long or six feet long.'

Frankly, they shouldn't care even if she is losing. Sania Mirza kept on wearing short skirts on court along with tee shirts that sometimes carried slogans. One said simply: 'I'm Cute.' Said another: 'I'm old enough to know better but still too young to care.' Care she did, however, and in her hometown, Hyderabad, dressed demurely.

Fortunately, her dresses did provoke that fatwa but didn't lead to violence. The clerics have every right under the Constitution to express a dissenting view on her sense of propriety. Under Article 19, they have the freedom of expression even to issue a fatwa and they should thank the founding fathers for allowing us all to enjoy that right in this country. However, under the same article, they have no right to call for any violent action, which they didn't. Perhaps Sania's nationwide popularity proved to be a winner in her favour, just as Shah Rukh Khan's adulation by the masses discouraged the Shiv Sena from taking things too far when they tried to stop the screening of his film.

However, violence against women remains a distinctive scar on the face of our democracy. In 1998, the National Crime Records Bureau reported that the growth rates of crimes against women would surpass the population's growth rate by 2010. At the time of writing, the latest statistics are not out, but the trend has subsisted. The reported rise in crimes against women might, however, have one positive side: an increasing number of women are breaking their silence to record complaints.

That is a welcome development. Plenty of data and literature are available on the frequency of rapes and beating of women and widespread gender bias in India. Detailing such information is not in the subject area of this essay. However, in such statistics, we can discover revealing indicators of the attitudes of Indian males and females when it comes to violence against women, especially violence at home.

A 2001 United Nations report, *Women In India*, lists a number of reasons for domestic violence and concludes:

'Violence against women within families is often justified and condoned as being necessary to establish men's authority over women, to "discipline" them and to punish them for derelictions of duty.' The problem is that such justification is supported not only by men 'but often by women themselves'.

The reasons listed for men being violent against women at home range from 'House not well managed', through 'Economic constraints' and 'Children not well cared for', to 'Meals not well prepared' and 'Meals not ready on time'. Interestingly, the last two reasons scored highest as the leading sources of violent male anger.

Education appears to play a significant role in determining women's levels of tolerance towards violence. Those who had high school education or more were far less tolerant of violence at the hands of their husbands. In Andhra Pradesh, for example, the proportion of illiterate women who justified husbands beating wives was a staggering 83 per cent; for high school graduates, the figure dropped to 62 per cent. At the national level, the figures were similar for cases of reported abuse. In 81 per cent of the cases, the husbands were illiterate; in the cases of men who had been through secondary education, the figure dropped dramatically to 41 per cent.

Clearly, education is a key factor in determining male as well as female attitudes towards violence against women. However, education by itself is not sufficient. Its quality, specifically its liberal quotient, counts a lot in a country where centuries of treating women as secondary human beings have solidified attitudes up and down the line.

Take a survey of 109 judges conducted in 1996 by the civil society organization Sakshi. The judges interviewed gave their attitudes towards violence against women:

- 48 per cent believed that there were certain occasions when it was justifiable for a husband to slap his wife;
- 74 per cent believed that the preservation of the family should be the woman's primary concern, even if she faced violence;
- 50 per cent believed that child sexual abuse was not common;
- 68 per cent believed that 'provocative' clothes were an invitation to sexual assault;
- 55 per cent believed that the moral character of a woman was relevant in cases of sexual abuse.

We should note that the Supreme Court has begun to apply principles of equality to issues of violence against women. From cases of sexual harassment at the workplace to matters of child custody and physical abuse at home, the court has ruled in important instances in favour of women. But then the Supreme Court of India takes a lot of initiatives that are proactive attempts from the top to change persisting realities. The fact is that far too many Indians see violence against women as often justifiable.

Oppression of women and their subordinate status mark out a society as inferior to the one that ensures full freedom and equality to women and does not discriminate between men and women in the exercise of rights. India, despite having had a woman prime minister and despite being a lot better than many other developing nations in offering its women legal equality of status, has some way to go before its women can claim true equality with men.

Seven

CHOKING EXPRESSION

Delivering the keynote address at the annual India Today Conclave in New Delhi in March 2010, Salman Rushdie said: 'Freedom is not a tea party. It has to be strongly argued. Disagreement with whoever wants to stifle your freedom has to be strongly fought. You have to shout at the frontier to protect your borders.'

He was making his first public comment on the situation of the artist M.F. Husain. He thought it strange that the Indian government was allowing Husain to be effectively banished from the country. 'Husain's plight is a distress. It is scurrilous, shameful. He is a loss to India. And ugliest is the language being used against him. He is even being jeered at for being old. This is a proud face of a philistine India.'

Rushdie regretted that a 'culture of complaint', which wasn't around earlier, seemed to have taken over India. 'In matters of culture, the mob rules. That is the tragedy.'

Some of us feel exactly the same. Here we are not talking about Hindu India or Muslim India. It is secular India we are anxious about.

When in March 2010 I wrote a column in *The Times of India* wondering how secular India came to such a pass that its greatest contemporary painter could no longer feel safe to return home and had taken up the citizenship of another nation, the responses I received were mostly from hostile e-mail and letter writers, many of whom appeared to be Hindus upset with Husain's depiction of goddesses in the nude. Some accused me of writing nonsense. Others implied that secularists had no understanding of the feelings of the religious-minded. One response, however, impressed me.

It advised, in a spelling form commonly used in text messages: 'Simply don't read or c it.' That was a sentence taken from my column in which I had suggested that if you were upset with any book or painting, 'simply don't read or see it.' That would be in the spirit of allowing free expression to both the writer or painter and yourself.

Clearly, this responder to the article had accepted my basic argument. He had advised others not to read the column because, in his view, it was not worth looking at or worse. His simple message was an ideal response to a view he had found distasteful. That is not to say that the others who had responded negatively were reacting inappropriately. Not at all, they too were doing the right thing by strongly expressing their disagreement in writing. This particular critic had, however, captured the essence of how to exercise our constitutionally guaranteed right to free expression.

Even so, that apparently simple principle is neither widely understood nor practised. Neither is the alternative, which is that if you feel up to it, disagree with the writer or the artist or the speaker by expressing yourself in as strong a language as you might consider appropriate, either in writing or in speech. You could gather a group of like-minded people to protest against that writer or artist; you could take the person to court for hurting your feelings and see whether your complaint stands under the law, as Husain's critics have done; or you could take your complaint to Parliament.

In short, under a democratic constitution you have several means at your disposal to express your outrage or anger, so long as you don't disturb public order or destroy property or threaten to hurt or kill someone. That is to say, disagree within the law.

Some have interpreted this freedom to mean that they should be allowed to burn a book or even the national flag in protest. Though this may be highly provocative to others, it should be considered a legitimate democratic action so long as it is done peacefully and safely.

Burning an effigy or a copy of a book or painting to express one's anger is common in India. What you cannot do under the law is burn the original painting or book, because that would amount to attacking property, private or public, or physically harm the person whose effigy you would like to burn. For those who are upset with the concept of an Indian nation for one reason or another, burning the national flag is a symbolic gesture of protest. Problems arise when the burning is a mere prelude to other, often wanton, acts of violence. That is where democratic freedom ends.

Can freedom of expression be without any limit? As is obvious from what is argued above, the answer is 'No'. Limits are imposed by the parameters of a democratic nation's constitution, by laws and specified circumstances under which freedom can be restrained. Thus, when someone, in a deliberate effort to dupe people and thus create panic, shouts 'Fire!' in a packed auditorium when there is none, he or she is clearly misusing freedom. That person is making a false statement in circumstances that could lead to chaos, injury or death, and is therefore liable for prosecution.

A book or painting that offends some people's sensibilities does not do that. The social disharmony that might come about as a result of a section of the people being upset is not created by the writer or the artist but by the pattern and intensity of the manner in which those sections express their outrage. The artist is not shouting 'Fire' in a closed public hall. The people who are protesting may be violating the law if they are violent or destructive.

We must remain free to express our views within the reasonable limits set by a democratic constitution, otherwise what is democracy for? Unfortunately, many in India do not appreciate this fundamental requirement of democracy, because so many are hostage to religious beliefs that often merge into bigotry. In an avowedly secular nation, you might assume it should be routinely possible to keep religious hatreds away from public policy and affairs of the state.

Unfortunately, that's not the case in India. The problem may lie in our peculiar interpretation of secularism.

The French intellectual, André Malraux, once asked Nehru what had been his greatest difficulty since India had gained independence, writes Ramchandra Guha in *India After Gandhi*. Nehru replied: 'Creating a state by just means.' A moment later, he added: 'Perhaps, too, creating a secular state in a religious country.'

The difficulty continues. Secularism in India has been an unstated assumption in its Constitution from the start and a stated part of that document's preamble since 1976. However, the extent of its success continues to be debated and forms one of the major fault lines in the landscape of Indian political ideologies, as we have seen.

Is secularism at all possible in its true form in a deeply religious country such as India? Those who say it is unsuited to the fabric of a religious country and should, therefore, be abandoned as an ideal are at least consistent in their position. Problems arise with the position of those who argue that a country like India must be secular but, as they try to implement secularism, feel compelled to dilute the concept. That dilution is passed off in India as merely another form of what some call 'non-Western' secularism; in fact, it is unique to this country, conditioned by circumstances in which the nation was born and survives. It is neither secularism as it is understood and practised in other nations that profess to be secular nor does it fit the definition.

Secularism grew out of historical circumstances in Europe, though it was enshrined for the first time in a constitution not in Europe but in the United States in 1791. Thomas Jefferson referred to the Establishment Clause in the first amendment to the US Constitution as a 'wall of separation' between the state and religion. Since then, several nations have followed that ideal.

Secularism has nothing against private religious beliefs or an individual's pursuit of religion. It is nevertheless a creed that has been historically locked in combat with religious power. A thread that runs through various definitions of secularism is that it entails scepticism of religious doctrine and rules out the use of public funds for religious education; it supports the separation of religious power from matters concerning the state, such as daily governance and the determination of public policy.

To elaborate what we discussed briefly earlier, the pursuit of secularism has historically involved attempts to establish an autonomous sphere of knowledge purged of supernatural, apocalyptic, or faith-based presuppositions. It seems to have begun in Europe, with the seeds of the idea being actually planted by religious scholars known as the Scholastics. That is not surprising, because the more you pursue knowledge through the accumulation of information based on evidence, the more likely you are to elevate reason at the cost of blind belief. That does not mean you inevitably abandon religion but it does mean an attempt to separate the sphere of faith from fields of knowledge. Reason can operate only in the realm of verifiable experience, not in the supernatural world.

Over time, secularism came to be identified with the pursuit of scientific knowledge. The growth of Protestantism and capitalism, with consequent alterations in the structure of political power in Europe, helped evolve secular state power separately from, and in opposition to, ecclesiastical power. Secularism in the philosophical sphere was a revolt against theological and metaphysical absolutes; in the political sphere, it was by its very definition a separation of religion from political life leading to the establishment of the state as an independent and contending source of power.

Thus, strict secularism requires that the state does not concern itself with religious practices and institutions; that although it should permit the pursuit of religious belief it should not associate itself with any particular religion; and that it must not discriminate between citizens on the basis of their religious beliefs. At least that is how the concept evolved in Europe and then in the rest of the world. Apart, that is, from India.

An argument some in India advance is that this country is simply too religious for the 'Western' brand of secularism to be viable. That, however, is an argument that could have been applied to every country in Europe during secularism's historical ascent and can be used in the case of a number of modern nations. The US, for example, is a deeply religious nation but its state, as well as important civil society groups, have over the years made the practice of secularism one of its fundamental tenets of public life. Debates continue over how far the state should go in enforcing the principle. Many conservatives resent what they see as an intrusion of the state in their domain of private Christian belief and would like religious doctrine to be taught in public schools or have religious symbols, such as crucifixes or tablets bearing the Ten Commandments, set up on public property. By and large, however, a majority of Americans firmly support secularism in practice.

When it comes to life in the private sphere, the state stands aside respectfully. Most American Christians – some surveys say as many as 80 per cent – attend church regularly. The US Constitution does not describe the nation as Christian. People of other faiths attend mosques, monasteries and temples of their choice. They are free to display religious symbols on their property and on their bodies. Wearing a hijab or a turban to school is not against the law in the US.

In France, they see it differently. The French state has banned the display of religious symbols, such as the the hijab, in public schools because the French practise a stricter form of secularism than the Americans. They place emphasis on French republicanism, which can have various meanings but includes a sense of what it should mean to be a 'French' national. That implies acceptance by immigrants of an overarching culture that involves speaking French as well as dropping most of the immigrants' distinguishing identities. Since the French state is secular, acceptance of republican virtues means not overtly displaying religious identities in public life.

Thus, the implementation of secular policies can have some flexibility in practice, as long as the state and religion remain more or less separate in the realm of governance and public policy. Whether the state, in active pursuit of the secular principle, should seek to undermine religious belief and promote reason through its educational and cultural policies is a matter on which different states take different positions. However, most versions of secularism in practice require the state to maintain a distance from religion.

Perhaps even more than France, a country that takes secularism as a fundamental condition of its constitutional make-up is Turkey. The Turkish military has intervened a few times to ensure the continuance of the secular character of the nation, as stipulated by the founder of modern Turkey, Kemal Ataturk, notwithstanding the fact that Islam is the religion of most of its citizens. With a pro-Islamic regime in power in Ankara, the government's apparent inclination towards religiosity generates recurring differences with the army's advocacy of uncompromising secularism.

To understand how Indian secularism is different, I shall mainly rely on Neera Chandhoke's account of its evolution in the *Oxford Companion to Politics in India*.

To summarize what she wrote, the progress of the nationalist movement against British colonialism had, by the early twentieth century, politicized religious identities. When Gandhi arrived to assume a leadership role, he realized that if he was to initiate a mass movement he would have to tackle the problem of politicization of religious identities, evident in the formation of the Muslim League or the Hindu Mahasabha. He searched around for an idea that could bring people together, even if they subscribed to different faiths. That's when he came up with the doctrine of '*sarva dharma sambhava*' or 'equality of all religions'. In this way, he laid the seed of the Indian mutation of secularism.

Given his own religiosity, Gandhi found it to be a

convenient principle that could bring people together while recognizing the value of religion in their lives. He was, however, not promoting secularism but a principle of tolerance, which he did not see at variance with his self-awareness as a religious Hindu.

Nehru saw the issue differently. He was uneasy with the primal passions that religious identities evoked, and saw secularism initially as a viable option. To him, secularism meant that the state would not be affected by religious considerations in conducting public affairs or in implementing public policy. For a while, he continued to subscribe to the formal definition of secularism as it was universally understood.

Gradually, Nehru felt compelled to moderate his view. Sporadic communal rioting that eventually erupted in the conflagration of the Partition massacre suggested to him that religious feelings, often in an extremely violent form, were a part of Indian politics. It would be politically impractical for him to ignore this reality. He began to move with the passage of time closer to the Gandhian version of secularism. By the time he became prime minister of independent India, he had forsaken formal secularism.

Secularism for him no longer meant primarily the separation of religion from the state or the discouragement of religion in any form. In *Jawaharlal Nehru: An Anthology,* Sarvepalli Gopal quotes the prime minister defining secularism: 'Some people think that it means something opposed to religion. That obviously is not correct. What it means is that it is a state which honours all faiths equally and gives them equal opportunities.' The state, he adds, does not allow itself to be attached to one faith or religion, which then becomes a state religion.

Freedom of religion was already assured by Article 25 of the Constitution, and was not a principle that diverged from the basic tenets of secularism. For Nehru, however, a secular state would not only allow freedom of religion, and the lack of religion, for all, it would respect all faiths. In Neera Chandhoke's reading, Nehru's understanding of the idea meant that secularism in the Indian context 'added one more dimension to the generic concept of secularism: not only the recognition of faith, but the equal treatment of all faiths'. Alternatively, we might argue that it was not secularism at all but a politically determined advocacy of tolerance in a multi-religious republic.

Nehru's view, which was an adaptation of Gandhi's, came to dominate the Indian understanding of secularism. In subsequent years no one, save perhaps a few academics and intellectuals, insisted on erecting a wall of separation between religion and politics in India. Even the courts followed Nehru's interpretation.

But the question is: what does 'equal treatment of all religions' mean in practice? The argument is not settled, even though most scholars and jurists seem to agree that in India secularism would have to mean something other than creating a wall of separation between religion and the state. Religion is too deeply embedded in Indian life, some argue; any attitude of indifference to religion on the part of the state will not work. Even if you accept that logic – which I don't, simply because other deeply religious societies have chosen to follow the generic interpretation of secularism with a fair degree of success – you are still left with several questions about Indian secularism.

What makes it complicated is the fact that one religious group, in this case the Hindu community, is numerically and culturally dominant, which often makes minority groups feel vulnerable to assimilation. In that case, is it alright to allow concessions to these minorities to help them avoid assimilation? If so, it doesn't remain 'equal treatment', does it?

Thanks to the wishy-washy nature of Indian secularism in theory and practice, the Indian state has over the decades merely succeeded in reaffirming the maxim that you can't please everybody every time. As mentioned earlier, the Shah Bano case of 1985 showed up in a harsh light the dilemma created by India's peculiar secularism. When the state high court ruled that as a divorced woman Shah Bano was entitled to receive alimony, her erstwhile husband moved the Supreme Court, arguing that he was not obliged to pay her any maintenance expenses beyond a traditional three-month period of 'iddat'. The Supreme Court upheld the high court's ruling and called upon the government to enact a uniform civil code under Article 44 of the Constitution.

The Muslim ulema voiced strong opposition on the ground that the judgment amounted to a disregard for personal laws based on the sharia, which was divinely ordained and could not be subject to an earthly court's jurisdiction. Thousands of Muslims marched on the streets to express their anger. Rajiv Gandhi's Congress government, with an eye on the Muslim vote, passed a law in Parliament exempting Muslim women from the constitutional provision granting women the right to receive alimony.

Liberals, feminists and leftists demonstrated widely against the new law. They were joined by the right, with the BJP arguing that any personal law of a minority group must be subject to a uniform civil code, a need reiterated by the Supreme Court.

While the BJP's stand may have been driven by its ideological position that called for an abolition of minority identities, the right, the left and liberal intellectuals were on firm ground in this episode. When in the Shah Bano case religious laws of a particular community came in the way of general social advancement, in this instance gender justice, the state should have taken a firm stand, especially as it had the clear backing of the judiciary. But, no, the state gave in to minority demands stoked by self-serving Islamic clerics. The government's weak response appeared all the more abject as, in an earlier phase of the republic, the state had intervened to change certain customs of the Hindu community in a quest for social progress.

In my view, secularism is not exactly the separation of religion from politics but is the separation of religion from the state, or, to express it in another way, it is erecting a wall between religious affairs and the affairs of the state. Religion, especially organized religion, generates its own politics as does the state, which rests on a political process. What a constitutionally secular state has to do is to disallow the influence of religious politics in public affairs and policy making or policy implementation. Thus, when a brand of majoritarian politics was leading up to the wrecking of the Babri mosque, the state should have felt constitutionally obliged to intervene at an appropriate time in the interest of both preserving public order and preventing the destruction of public property. Similarly, in the Shah Bano case, the state should have simply shrugged to say that secular courts had decided in favour of a divorced woman in accordance with the law and the state had no intention of usurping the judiciary's territory. That is how other secular nations respond to demands of extra-constitutional concessions from religious groups. Why do we need to reinvent the wheel by debating competing contortions of secularism? If it can work for so long with a high degree of success in a deeply religious and argumentative nation such as the US, why can't it work in India?

It can't because the state has been unwilling to make it work. It has increasingly shied away from countering religious politics with strong and saleable secular politics. It wasn't always so. As we have noted, in the early years of the republic, when it mustered support in Parliament and outside for the passage of marriage and succession laws for Hindus, the state was willing to argue its case. True, even at that time the government did not think it possible to introduce a uniform civil code and drew away from changing Islamic personal practice. Even so, leaders like Nehru and Ambedkar were ardent secularists who only reluctantly agreed to hold in abeyance any change in Muslim personal law bearing in mind the bitterness of Partition and India's credibility to its minorities. It was when Nehru began to move away from his understanding of secularism to a Gandhian interpretation of the concept that secularism in the Indian context acquired an exceptional meaning.

It would be accurate to call India a tolerant nation in principle rather than a truly secular one. Unfortunately, tolerance does not work uniformly in practice. While each religious group demands and usually obtains tolerance for itself, it does not always grant the same consideration to other groups. Tolerance for our kind of folks but not for any other seems to be the norm. Even so, the idea of India is founded on an acceptance of tolerance by every religious, ethnic, cultural and linguistic group. Without that tolerance in practice, it cannot exist indefinitely.

There are, in my view, two ways in which the Indian state can support and promote that tolerance. One is by continuing its current version of secularism with a much stronger determination to maintain law and order as befitting a hard state, to use Gunnar Myrdal's term. The state must intervene firmly, and sometimes in proactive anticipation, to prevent religious emotions from spilling over into violence.The other option is to reconstruct the secularism that Ambedkar and Nehru had originally envisaged for an emerging nation. It would be a secularism that would not offer to treat all religious demands equally, but will consciously and rigorously maintain an equidistance from all religions. In other words, the state would move away from being all things to all sects and build a wall separating religious affairs from its own affairs in the public domain. Simultaneously, it would promote the kind of tolerance on which this secular-liberal democracy should for viability base itself. Secular but tolerant reason must replace competitive religious fervour. After all, if religion is not downgraded from its centrality in political life, the survival of the nation will be at stake. A unique experiment in nation building might then be endangered.

Eight

INTERPRETING SECULARISM

Is secularism a European phenomenon and, therefore, irrelevant to India in its Western-inspired form? Can a society steeped in faith and rituals ever erect a wall to separate religion from the state? Isn't it impractical to attempt to transplant secularism in its historically evolved Western sense in the very different Indian soil?

Several intellectuals and academicians, who are not religious fanatics by any stretch of the imagination, have cautioned against implementing 'Western' secularism in India. Ashis Nandy has rejected it outright as a legitimate policy option and has argued for the recognition of religious identities in the public sphere. In his view, secularism, by banishing religion to the periphery of society, allows the state to dominate individual and collective lives. At the same time, it inhibits dialogue between the religious and political spheres to the detriment of both. When a secular public space is populated by morally crippled and truncated personalities, thanks to the absence of the positive impact of religion on their lives, religious fanatics step in to use religion to serve their narrow ends. To avoid this outcome, a tradition of tolerance must be revived, feels Nandy, not through religion as ideology but through faith in a pure form. 'Faith is more lived out than articulated and tolerance or forgiveness is given expression in the actualities of living, not in ideological or even theological propositions,' says Nandy in *An Anti-Secularist Manifesto*.

Sociologist T.N. Madan believes that 'secularism in South Asia as a generally shared credo of life is impossible'. A vast majority of people living in the subcontinent are followers of one religion or another and define their lives through faith, whereas in Christian Europe developments such as the Reformation helped secularization and an accompanying privatization of religion, he says. In his opinion, religion in this region establishes the place of individuals in society and gives meaning to their lives; it would, therefore, be foolish and arrogant to impose secularism on the faithful. The religious should be given a stature equal to the secular.

These are views of highly respected and widely published academicians. The problem, in my careful dissent, is that they skirt the factual sequence of the historical evolution of secular ideas, leaning towards an anti-modern world-view (Nandy is a known critic of modernity) and assuming a form of rigid Indian exceptionalism.

True, secularism grew as an idea in the West out of specific historical circumstances. It is, however, now a part of world history, much as Indian mathematics or

Chinese, Arab and Greek advancements are profoundly part of human development. Many concepts and ideas emerged from Europe's sociopolitical turmoil in the last millennium, starting with the Renaissance, followed by the Reformation, the Enlightenment, the Age of Reason and the scientific revolution, to say nothing of colonialism, war and untold destruction that occurred in the process. Capitalism, socialism, nationalism, republicanism, constitutional democracy and secularism may have all grown out of European circumstances over four or five centuries, but are widely accepted today as global ideas that almost all aspiring nations have adopted partially or fully. If secularism is a concept that cannot work in India, whereas it can work in other religious-minded societies, we might as well argue, as some do, that republican democracy cannot work either. Alternatively, let's abandon all modern concepts as they are unfamiliar to Indian society, apart from being unsuitably foreign and apparently impracticable. Indeed, why write a constitution? In a pre-modern and poorly literate society, is such a document of any practical use?

Obviously, critics of secularism do not go quite so far, as they would readily acknowledge. They themselves are as much products of the revolution of reason in the modern world, starting from Europe, while the methods of criticism they employ are derived from that advancement in logical reasoning. They are supporters of freedom and human rights, which both emanated as ideals from a rising recognition of the importance of personal dignity and individual rights in modernizing societies. Secularism is an inseparable part of that same revolution of reason. It played a critical role in shearing unquestionable religious authority from political power.

Many of the nation's founding leaders well understood the need. Gandhi, Gopal Krishna Gokhale, C. Rajagopalachari, Nehru, and Ambedkar were avowed secularists. However, as we have noted, their understanding of how secularism should be implemented in a deeply religious and multi-faith society differed. Ambedkar's view counted a lot because he played such a key role in devising the Indian Constitution, and he steadfastly held on to his interpretation of secularism in response to those who wanted to dilute the concept. For instance, Article 44 of the Constitution asks the state to endeavour to implement a uniform civil code, yet when it came up in Parliament, several members, many of them Muslim, agitated against it. Ambedkar argued firmly that if personal laws were to be saved for particular communities, 'in social matters we will come to a standstill'. He argued that in order to advance much needed social reform in a traditional society, where there were many inequities and widespread discrimination, any comprehensive influence of religion on life had to be curtailed.

When tackling a vigorous and widely expressed opposition of Hindu traditionalists to reforming personal law, the new Indian state handled the process competently. Although it took a few years of debate and political management, the state succeeded, under Nehru's leadership, in passing the relevant Acts in Parliament. However, as we saw earlier, it shied away from touching Muslim personal law. Equal treatment of religions, as promised in the Indian version of secularism, did not work in practice.

Indian secularism does retain two important features of the real thing. The Indian state is not theocratic, and Article 25 of the Constitution gives freedom of religion to all citizens. The state, however, intervenes periodically in religious matters and its intervention sometimes leads to unequal and discriminatory treatment of religions. In order to protect minorities from their fear of assimilation, the state elevates group identities above those of individual identities. Group rights often trump individual rights of citizens. The state does not try to ensure that group rights are arrived at or generated democratically; usually the claims of a clergy are taken to represent the group's view in a manner which seems to go directly counter to the citizen's ability to practise both freedom of expression and freedom of religion.

The Supreme Court of India has played an active role in interpreting secularism. The activist role of the court has generated both support and considerable criticism. In a fine, scholarly account of the court's role in interpreting our constitutional right to freedom of religion and its influence on the discourse of secularism and nationalism, Ronojoy Sen, a former colleague in *The Times of India,* has demonstrated how the Indian version of secular governance differs from that of other secular democracies and how the Supreme Court has often intervened to define and demarcate religion and religious freedom. In his meticulously researched book, *Articles of Faith: Religion, Secularism and the Indian*

Supreme Court, Sen traces the various legal and conceptual controversies surrounding the court's activism.

By examining decisions and interventions from 1951 to the present, Sen detects patterns in the court's opinion making, though he clarifies that no linear thinking is evident. Two factors that seem to have exerted influence are, first, the personalities of dominant judges, usually serving chief justices or judges who would later become chief justices; and, second, the political climate prevalent in different phases of independent India's history. In the early 1950s, the courts seemed to give considerable freedom to religious denominations in line with the constitutional provision of the state giving free play to all religions. This changed in the 1960s.

With P. B. Gajendragadkar becoming the dominant voice on the bench, the 1960s marked the beginning of a role for the state in regulating and administering temples. The court seemed to believe increasingly in a need for social engineering and its views can be seen as a product of Nehruvian rationalism. Sen refers to the political scientist James Scott to describe this approach as one of 'high modernism':

> Some key components of Scott's formulation of modernism are supreme confidence in progress and a rationalist understanding of the world. The faith reposed by high modernism in progress and rationality implies a 'truly radical break' with history and tradition.

Sen proceeds to quote the conservative philosopher and political theorist Michael Oakshott, who defines a rationalist as someone who stands 'for independence of mind on all occasions, for thought free from obligation to any authority, save the authority of "reason"'. As he is an enemy of authority, and of prejudice, the merely habitual or customary has no value for him and the rationalist can easily engage in 'destruction and creation'. Thus, for Oakshott, a rationalist is habitually contentious and against tradition.

Adds Sen, in apparent approval of Scott and Oakshott: 'Indeed, Gajendragadkar, and his intellectual mentor Jawaharlal Nehru, fit Scott's description of progressive elites who desire the use the power of the state to "bring about enormous changes in people's habits, work, living patterns, moral conduct and world-view"'. To members of the Nehruvian elite, high modernism had appeal because they saw themselves 'as responsible for nation building and social transformation'. In Scott's understanding: 'Where this intelligentsia conceives of its mission as the dragging of a technically backward, unschooled, subsistence-oriented population into the twentieth century, its self-assigned cultural role as educator of its people becomes doubly grandiose.'

There is merit to the argument that many judges of the Supreme Court, as 'high' modernists and Nehruvian rationalists, intervened too much in religious matters. Their intentions may have been sincere in fighting superstition and religious rigidity but in some cases, as Sen points out, they ended up defining Hinduism in a manner that could have helped religious ideologues give a legal patina to their take on Hinduism. The contradiction of judges in a secular nation interpreting religion did not show up very much as long as the court confined itself to Hindu texts and traditions. However, when a judge took on Islamic law in the Shah Bano case mentioned earlier, as Justice Y.V. Chandrachud did, it led to massive public protest.

Further, while it is perfectly in line with secular intent for the courts and the state to fight against religious superstition and irrationalities and pass or enforce laws to abolish social practices such as untouchability, the Supreme Court also allowed the state to become involved in managing religious institutions, even regulating rituals and modes of worship. 'The involvement of the state in religious institutions flew in the face of the Nehruvian assumption that the domain of religion would gradually shrink,' writes Sen. Political scientist Pratap Bhanu Mehta, in *The Telegraph* of 4 March 2003, correctly points out: 'The Indian state has used state power to consolidate Hindu identity in more ways than one can list. [It] created a territorially unified body of Hindu law, transcending numerous regional divisions. Supreme Court judges not only promulgate public purposes, they act as authoritative interpreters of Hindu religion...' The state, he adds, ran thousands of temples across the country, appropriated in the name of social reform and financial propriety.

It is obvious that a need for accommodation in multicultural, multiethnic, and multi-religious India makes the constitutional provision of secularism somewhat nebulous. It makes the job of the courts in India more difficult than in those secular republics where the separation of religion and state has been more rigorously maintained. In Sen's view: 'As we look ahead to what appears to be a period of increasing uncertainty, where religion and religious identity will continue to play a prominent role, the Court should rethink its language of uniformity in favour of one that is more accommodative of religious and legal pluralism.' Else, he warns, matters of religion and faith could be hijacked by Hindu nationalists or Islamic radicals.

In other words, in conceding the reality of the Indian situation today we may have to opt for a continuation of a form of accommodative tolerance as the essence of Indian secularism and forget, for the time being at least, about erecting a wall of separation between religion and the state. It is indeed late in the day to revive the intentions of modernists like Ambedkar, Nehru and Rajaji. That does not mean the intentions were wrong or unsuitable for India but that in the past six decades, the Indian state has allowed the distance between state and religion to shrink to a point where any concept other than an enlightened tolerance on the part of the state towards every religious community can work. However, it will not be secularism as it is recognized in other nations; it will be ceding secular ground to the power of religion over people's minds on yet another plea of Indian exceptionalism, that secularism can work in the West but not in India.

As I have discussed before, by that argument we should not be attempting in the first place to create one unified nation out of India's immense diversity. If we follow the claims of Indian exceptionalism to their logical end, we could argue that caste or linguistic divisions or sensitivity towards myriad sub-nationalisms or the reality of competing religious emotions must trump any argument for indivisible nationhood, which is also a concept that historically emerged from Europe in the modern era. For that matter, we should not even think of trying out republican democracy in hierarchical India or in any territory where circumstances were likely to be radically altered by products of 'high modernism'. Why instal elaborate legal systems to be enforced by courts of law? After all, the notion of individual rights that can be debated from competing angles emerged from the master idea of habeas corpus, which was not only a secular concept emerging out of political and economic circumstances, but formed an integral part of the very evolution of 'reason', a development so disdained by anti- and postmodernists.

If James Scott believes that a section of the 'high' modernist intelligentsia sees its mission as 'the dragging of a technically backward, unschooled, subsistence-oriented population into the twentieth century', and that this self-assigned role is 'grandiose', we could equally argue that another section of the same intelligentsia, which, like Scott, is imbued with a grand sense of value-neutral relativism, seems to want that same subsistence-oriented population to be left alone to devise each traditional community's answer to life's challenges. In other words, do not interfere with time-honoured values or identities; let people remain where they are. It sounds like a fair proposition until you ask whether it is not equally presumptive of what people might want for themselves and their children's futures, or whether we ought in that case to reverse the entire progressive civilizational enterprise in order to return to a pre-modern life that, we could agree with Hobbes, was nasty, brutish and short.

To be fair, that's not where the critics of modernism are

willing to go. For them, criticism can be an end in itself; alternative solutions are not theirs to suggest. With such an approach, secularism seems a relatively easy target to shoot at; democracy and republicanism are more complicated. When you are supposedly arguing on behalf of communities oppressed by the tyranny of reason or 'high' modernism, you might find it hard to take a position against democracy itself. Secularism is simpler to attack because defending the sanctity of religious identity or belief is not difficult in a world dominated by faith in one organized form or another. You can thus criticize godless secularism but you must be tender with religion for fear of causing offence.

In March 2010, the Geneva-based Human Rights Council (HRC) of the United Nations voted 20-17 for a motion that wants the 'defamation of religion' to be listed as an infringement of liberty. The Organization of the Islamic Conference (OIC), comprising fifty-six Muslim states and Palestine, has been trying lately to have the General Assembly and other UN bodies pass a resolution of that kind, reported *The Economist* of 3 April 2010. At the HRC, the margin by which the non-binding resolution was passed was smaller than earlier, which encouraged opponents of the resolution to hope that the next time such a motion was raised it wouldn't succeed.

The OIC wants the world to accept its position that religious faiths, like individuals, need protection. At first hearing, that sounds a reasonable demand, but it is not.

Critics of the OIC's campaign point out, first, that defamation legally means harming the reputation of a living person or entity; you cannot defame an idea or a religious leader who is no longer alive. Second, that kind of a resolution, if made binding by the UN, would help countries which use laws against blasphemy to criminalize dissent. The *Economist* illustrates the point by referring to blasphemy laws in Pakistan, where the police registered forty-one complaints of blasphemy in 2009. And in January 2011, the liberal governor of Punjab, Salmaan Taseer, was assassinated by his own bodyguard for trying to moderate the blasphemy law.

The communities worst affected by the blasphemy law are Ahmadiyas and Christians. As Ali Dayan Hasan, a researcher at Pakistan's Human Rights Watch, a non-government body, told the magazine: 'The most vulnerable people, that is religious minorities, continue to be charged with blasphemy.' People are rarely convicted, but when they are they receive long jail terms. In January 2009, five Ahmadiyas were charged and jailed for allegedly writing 'Prophet Muhammed' on the wall of a mosque toilet. In September that year, a Pakistani Christian was accused of throwing the Koran down a drain, when his offence was to fall in love with a Muslim woman. He was jailed, where he died, allegedly tortured by the police.

The secretary-general of the OIC, Ekmeleddin Ihsanoglu, who was interviewed by the magazine, said: 'We are not against the freedom of expression, freedom of the press or civilized criticism. The target is to invite everybody to respect Islam.'

Once again, it seems a reasonable demand, but is it? Two

questions arise: First, why should 'everybody', including Christians, Hindus, Jews, Sikhs, atheists, and agnostics, be compelled to respect Islam, or any other faith, on the basis of a binding global resolution? Second, will Islamists feel equally obligated to respect all faiths or will bigots among them, like fanatics everywhere, continue to denigrate other religions?

Furthermore, will being supportive of the freedom of expression and of the press mean not being violent in protest against a Dutch cartoonist for drawing a caricature of a religious leader? Will the OIC then disallow fatwas to murder authors on charges of blasphemy? Would support for 'civilized criticism' include permitting Muslim feminists like, say, Ayan Hirsi Ali, to write books criticizing the oppression of women in Islamic societies? Alternatively, if such a resolution were indeed passed by the UN, would it prevent Hindu fanatics from persecuting an artist like M.F. Husain? Are such doubts of no concern to the OIC, which seeks respect for only its version of Islam?

One problem with all such moves, supposedly to protect religion as a genre, is embedded in the word 'religion'. Demanding respect for religion is akin to wanting respect for, say, politics. Within politics there are political parties and ideologies contesting one another across the world. Asking for a generic respect for politics is, therefore, meaningless. Similarly, demanding respect for 'religion' is of no practical use given the world's numerous faiths, sects and the often very bitter conflicts they wage amongst themselves. Inter-religious as well as intra-religious violence marks many of the darkest chapters in human history. Just the act of raising such a demand suggests that believers want a level of specially sensitive treatment for religion and faith that they feel must be above that given to secular reason or science.

Apart from being offensive to atheists and agnostics – we are a relatively insignificant minority in global society – such pleas ignore the state of religious belief in the world today. It may be fashionable to claim that all religions are beautiful and that their fundamentals or essentials are the same. It is sheer nonsense, however, to assert anything of the sort. Each religion claims its own true path to wisdom and opposes, explicitly or implicitly, similar claims of every other religion. That embedded source of conflict has in the past, and continues today, to generate the kind of violence that all religions insist they are doctrinally against because they are for peace, harmony and the brotherhood of humankind.

Stephen Prothero, a professor of religion in Boston University, who is no atheist, has written perceptively on the issue in his book *God is Not One: The Eight Rival Religions That Run the World*. He finds it odd that while no one argues that different economic systems or political regimes are one and the same, many scholars and popularizers of religion claim that religious rivals such as Hinduism and Islam, Judaism and Christianity are essentially the same and basically good. If that were true, there should be no real ground for violent disagreement between Hindus and Muslims or Catholics and Protestants or Muslims and Jews. As we all know, such is hardly the case. Religious belief systems are mutually and dogmatically exclusive. Every religion stakes its own claim to unchallenged truth, its particular vision of what life should be, and what afterlife has in store for us.

Like Gandhi, those who assert that various religions are different paths to the same goal do not deny that there are differences in dogma, rituals and institutions. A Buddhist or a Jain does not believe there is a god, a Hindu worships numerous gods, while Christians, Muslims and Jews insist there is only one god. Do these differences matter? No, say those who believe that religion is one common quest for the divine in which different approaches of the world's faiths grow out of one root. As Gandhi wrote to Nehru in a letter: 'The root of all religions is one and it is pure and all of them have sprung from the same source, hence all are equal.'

Even so, much of history is a tale of bitter fights over religious differences. Each religious sect points to the others as purveyors of a multitude of wrong beliefs. The Christian, for example, believes in 'salvation' from sin, laughs at theologies promoting multiple gods (but admires the wisdom of ancient Greeks who had many gods), and claims that Jesus is the son of God. The Jew and the Muslim, who share much of the same mythology, disagree strongly on the claim about God's son. The bloody results of such differences have haunted the world right up to the present, though no one is suggesting that all blame for violence in history can be laid at religion's door.

Nehru wrote in *An Autobiography* that religion, or at any rate organized religion, horrified him: 'Almost always it seems to stand for blind belief and reaction, dogma and bigotry, superstition and exploitation, and the preservation of vested interests.' He added: 'Organized religion, allying itself to theology and often more concerned with its vested interests than with things of the spirit, encourages a temper which is the very opposite to that of science. It produces narrowness and intolerance, credulity and superstition, emotionalism and irrationalism.' He was not against religion in every sphere of human society. As is usually the case with agnostics and atheists, and he was a self-declared disbeliever in a 'personal god', he would acknowledge the power, even the values, of religion in people's private lives.

In *The Discovery of India*, Nehru explained his position on religion when he wrote that religions had helped greatly in the development of humanity by laying down values and standards and pointing out principles for the guidance of human life. 'But with all the good they have done, they have also tried to imprison truth to set forms and dogmas, and encouraged ceremonials and practices which soon lose all their original meaning and become mere routine.'

The hard interpretation of secularism that some academicians detect in the Supreme Court's opinions can be traced directly to Nehru. As Ronojoy Sen details in the book cited earlier, Justice Gajendragadkar in particular saw the impact of religion on modern society in much the same way as Nehru, his intellectual guiding light. In his view, Indian society 'is still traditional. It leans on scriptures, beliefs and superstitions rather than on reason, experience and principles of modernism'. He was of the view that religion, as it was actually practised among the Hindu masses, tended to be reactionary in its outlook and sought to perpetrate the distinctions between castes and communities and sustain social inequality 'in all its nakedness'.

Neither he nor Nehru was against religion per se. For them, religion in an abstract, spiritual sense, and practised at a personal level away from the sphere of the state, was not out of sync with a secular polity. They visited places of worship and, on occasion, experienced wonder and even bliss. For them, as with other secularists, religion could provide a foundation of ethics in society and could be a source of serenity for individuals.

Gajendragadkar described Hinduism as a 'way of life' and not a religion like other faiths. In his out-of-court commentary he even said that the true nature of secularism under the Indian Constitution was fundamentally based on Hindu philosophy. He thought there existed in the Hindu tradition a tolerance of dissent, which made it particularly conducive to secularism. 'It is this characteristic catholicity and freedom which are the hallmark of Hindu philosophy, religion and culture; and it is this catholicity again, which is the basis of the spirit of tolerance in the positive sense, that is the special feature of Indian secularism,' wrote the judge.

That is not an understanding of Hinduism or the Hindu tradition with which a secularist like Amebdkar, a Dalit, would agree. To Dalits, who endured inhuman intolerance over centuries, Hinduism as a way of life followed the bedrock principle of tolerance, 'live and let live', in a stark sense: Brahmins, and other high castes, who occupied the peaks of society, allowed those at the bottom to live but only barely. No human dignity or generosity of spirit was evident in that hierarchical and fundamentally intolerant social structure. Hindu philosophy may preach tolerance or allow dissent to a few but Hinduism in real life offered no respite to any human who had the misfortune to be born in the wrong caste. Nothing in the spirit of Hindu philosophy could change that because philosophy and debate existed largely in the exclusive world of Brahmins, who were members of a destiny-determined club of information monopolists. It is hardly a tradition that is in harmony with secularism.

Elements of tolerance and instances of dissent exist to one degree or another in every religious order. Apart from the tolerance and social dissent preached by Jesus Christ and later disciples, the Scholastics of the twelfth and thirteenth centuries critically inquired into existing Christian dogma; Duns Scotus and William of Ockham took the questioning far enough for later chroniclers of philosophy to trace the roots of secular thought and subsequent British empiricism in their inquiries. In Islam, a tradition of *ijtihad* produced philosophers like Ibn Rushd and Ibn Sena, who revived and advanced the thoughts of ancient Greek philosophers, while a Sufi movement that preached a form of Islamic mysticism with tolerance exerted great influence on the Indian subcontinent. Although some Hindus claim Buddhism and Jainism as part of Hinduism, these are today separate religions and both schools of thought rest on an advocacy of universal tolerance. In short, Hinduism is not uniquely tolerant or permitting of dissent among the world's religious traditions, and a Supreme Court judge's claim that it fits in well with secularism cannot make it so.

Finding similarities between the Hindu way of life and the secularism that India had resolved for itself can also be seen as stoking the anxiety of minorities. That was what the creators of Pakistan had feared, that in a Hindu-dominated India secularism would be distorted and soft Hinduism would replace it. In fact, the Supreme Court's opinions and judgments on such matters have inadvertently ended up awarding a certificate of legitimacy to champions of Hindutva when they have argued that secularism in India is compatible with the Hindu tradition. Followers of other religions might disagree for all they are worth but that has not stopped ideologues of the Sangh Parivar from asserting that in India real secularism, as opposed to soft 'pseudo-secularism', is compatible with Hindutva.

It may no longer be politically feasible for India to attempt a return to the rigorous secularism once advocated by statesmen such as Ambedkar, Nehru and Rajaji, as well as by the Supreme Court. However, those in charge of the nation's direction can renew efforts to advance the core principle of a secular society, which is a proactive tolerance of different viewpoints, the corollary of which is protection of individual rights, ensuring freedom of expression, delegitimizing violence as a means of political or social disagreement, and channelizing dissent into sustained democratic behaviour.

To attempt that, the state would need to take stronger positions against religious excesses and fanaticism than it has so far. At the same time, it will have to deflate the role of religion in public life and try to move it more towards the private sphere.

Nine

RELIGION AND ILLIBERALISM

On a Saturday in early May 2010, a thirty-year-old American man of Pakistani origin parked a bomb-laden sport utility vehicle in a crowded area in New York's Times Square. Faisal Shahzad ran away from the vehicle but the bombs did not go off. Two alert street vendors saw smoke coming out of the SUV and informed the police, who went into action to defuse the explosives and save the lives of many walking about in the crowded square. Shahzad tried to flee the US but was apprehended at JFK airport. He reportedly confessed to the act of attempted terrorism, saying that anger against the US, of which he was a naturalized citizen, had driven him to it.

His anger grew after the US, in a stepped-up effort to combat terrorism emerging from Pakistan, began to deploy unmanned aircraft, or drones, to bomb places near his ancestral home. A burst of religious zeal apparently fuelled his anger. His transformation from a young suburban American family man to religious zealot is worth retelling. Shahzad's story is an instance of how religion can drive violent rage.

He moved to America as a student in the late 1990s. He belonged to a well-heeled family in Pakistan; his father was a retired air vice marshal and his family owned substantial property. After graduating from a university in Connecticut and acquiring an additional qualification in business management, he began working, initially in a cosmetic company and then with a financial firm. In 2004 he had an arranged marriage with Huma Mian, who was born in Colorado and studied in the University of Colorado in Boulder. At their wedding in Peshawar there was much gaiety and dancing. A wedding guest told *The New York Times* that at the time 'there was no sign of him being an extremist or, for that matter, he wasn't a bit religious'.

The couple bought a house in Shelton, Connecticut, for $275,000 and had children. A few months after the birth of their second child they packed up, stopped paying their home mortgage instalments, and apparently left the US for Pakistan. By then, Shahzad had quit his job at the financial firm and, according to acquaintances, had steadily begun developing a religious identity. A former classmate said he had noticed something different in Shahzad's personality from some time in 2009. He had become introverted and 'had a stronger religious identity, where he felt more opinionated about things'.

Faiz Ahmad, a friend from his village in Pakistan, told an interviewer from *The New York Times* that Shahzad's transformation was odd. 'The question is who has put Faisal in this path?' asked Ahmad. 'The Faisal with the beard that you see, he was not the old Faisal. He was like you, like me, handsome, liberal and an active person.'

Media accounts following his arrest speculated that money worries and a growing inability to meet his home mortgage payments may have contributed to an accumulating sense of frustration. However, at some point, frustration, whatever its source, seemed to have given way to anger against the US. He began watching militant Islamic videos and may have contacted radical clerics who advocated violence against America. Then he visited Waziristan to learn how to make bombs from the Pakistani Taliban, who later claimed to have planned the Times Square attack.

As with Major Nidal Hasan, the US army man who went on a shooting rampage in Fort Hood, Texas, to kill fellow soldiers in revenge for US attacks on Islamic nations, the transformation of an educated, middle-class, apparently well-adjusted American immigrant into an enraged, vengeful fanatic is an example of personal frustration or disappointment finding violent expression in religion. Violence may be a common characteristic among the religious as well as the irreligious or the secular. However, followers of all religions without exception insist that their faith is peaceful and that violent fanatics are either misguided folks or poor victims in search of justifiable redress against evil followers of other faiths.

That is because faith in any particular religion is a system of branded belief; all other brands are, by any particular faith's exclusivist definition, potentially misleading or evil or both. Reason, on the other hand, evolved to challenge faith and is generic in its evidence-based logic that carries within itself the seeds of disbelief and disproof.

That is why secular humanism is, in my view, a system of thought better suited to the sustainability and continuing creativity of humankind than any religious creed or syncretistic faith. However, by its very nature, secular humanism has to be based on the acceptance of democratic liberal values, and as such must allow space for religious belief and expression so long as it is conducted within the confines of democratic law and practice and not to the exclusion of other points of view. The pluralism such a secular society entails does not forbid religion; on the contrary, it guarantees space for religious practice both in the private sphere as well as in the public. It just requires religion to stay away from affairs of the state and vice versa.

As I acknowledged earlier, the form of secularism that requires vigilant separation between religion and the state may no longer be possible in India. The issue was in a way decided in the early years of the republic, with even an ardent secularist like Nehru succumbing to a perceived need to accommodate religion and allow the state to involve itself in religious matters. Moreover, job reservations for backward sections of society and preferential treatment in general for poor people became closely identified with caste and tribal identities and not primarily with economic conditions or fair access to opportunity. Affirmative action, desirable as it was and remains in any democracy striving for optimal equity in society, became overshadowed by quota reservations. It is extremely difficult now to correct course.

Therefore, in India secularism as a form of pluralistic tolerance has come to stay. However, to make it work in a religion-besotted nation entails an active role on the part of the state in promoting secular reason as the mode of discourse in public affairs and keeping religious faith as far away as possible from influencing policy and social choices. At a minimum, while treating religion with respect and guaranteeing protected space for faith in all its versions, the state can surely continue to argue vigorously against superstition, religious dogma and obscurantism through schools and colleges and by encouraging public debate through the media. To do that, a majority of political and social leaders will have to unequivocally accept, as did Nehru, Ambedkar and Rajaji in the early years of the republic, the primacy of reason in modern life. They must resist conceding demands that promote sectarian faith at the expense of secular reason; and debate the views of those relativist postmodern scholars who portray faith and reason to be equally valid. Otherwise, tolerance and democratic pluralism will have to cede ground to intolerance masquerading in the guise of religious belief.

To get a sense of what could happen to a nation when its founding definition is that of religion, take a look at our neighbouring state, Pakistan, whose early leaders were ambivalent about how to treat religion in its constitution, and even though a few wanted to, they could not ultimately create a secular edifice in which religion could enjoy a protected sanctuary away from the territory of the state and secular politics. The result is there for all to see and for a terrorized world to endure the consequences.

The story of Faisal Shahzad, recounted earlier, sparked off a flurry of questions around the globe: Why did he do it? What are the links between Islam and jihad? Importantly too, why does Pakistan figure so ominously in so many terror-related incidents around the world? The British authorities said some time ago that 70 per cent of terror events in their country had a link with Pakistan. We Indians can shake our heads in empathy; so can the Americans after a series of attempted cases of terrorism involving US citizens who became radicalized after hooking up with jihadi groups in Pakistan. What is it about Pakistan that provides jihadis with a hospitable ground for their activities? Is there something in its basic structure that has a design fault?

It appears that unquestioning belief creates a kind of mindset that blinds you to possible problems around you and in your system of belief that others can see. After Shahzad had been arrested, his parents in Pakistan understandably entered a period of shock. His father was a retired air vice marshal, who had brought up his children well and had sent Shahzad to the US precisely because he feared that Pakistan's poisoned atmosphere might contaminate his son's outlook. Many in Pakistan, however, refused to believe that there could be anything wrong in their society that would turn an upright young man like Shahzad into a would-be terrorist. A flood of conspiracy theories floated up to suggest that the affair was an American plot to defame Pakistan and Pakistanis. Shahzad in that view was an innocent victim.

Typical was the reaction of Iftikhar Ahmed, a relative of Shahzad and a retired air force officer. He told *The Washington Post* two weeks after the Times Square incident: 'We sent a clean and innocent boy to America. If he went bad in America, why don't you blame America instead of his family and his country?' Why his father had sent him to America in the first place wasn't a question to be asked or answered.

Writing in *The Washington Post* on 9 May 2010, Fareed Zakaria asked why Pakistan remained a terrorist hothouse at a time when jihadists were losing support elsewhere in the Muslim world. 'The answer is simple,' he said. 'From its founding, the Pakistani government has supported and encouraged jihadi groups, creating an atmosphere that has allowed them to flourish.' Unsurprisingly, it's a conclusion with which many thoughtful Pakistanis, who form a vocal but tiny minority, agree.

Inaugurating a conference in Washington in early May on 'Competing Religious Narratives in Pakistan: Can Islam Be an Agency for Peace?', Husain Haqqani, Pakistan's erudite ambassador to the US, offered a strikingly candid set of observations. He began by quoting from an April 1957 essay by Hasan Suhrawardy, the then prime minister, in which the veteran politician wondered, apparently in exasperation with Islamist ideologues, whether the insertion in the constitution of the adjective 'Islamic' to describe the state was meant in any way to be a sign of courage or moral excellence. Today, said Haqqani, the 'vision' thing is hardly discussed. Popular discourse in Pakistan is over trivialities and dominated by conspiracy theories while the violent religious assertions of a minority of Pakistan's population are taken by the ruling authorities as the accepted view of the nation.

Is Pakistan an ideological state or a nation state, asked the ambassador, making it clear that he stood with those who wanted it to be a nation in which secular politics formed the principal channel of discourse, and not a theocratic entity. 'Politics is the grand avenue of service to humanity,' he declared. Religious parties could have a legitimate role in politics, he added, but they must not have a veto over the direction in which the country is moving by threatening those who would support pluralism and democracy. 'Pakistan is not going to suffer because of open debate,' said Haqqani. 'Pakistan has suffered because it has not had open debate.'

Haqqani's speech was followed by similarly insightful and forthright presentations by, among others, two Pakistani intellectuals. Farzana Shaikh, who is with Chatham House in London, pleaded for the introduction of a minimal form of secularism in a rapidly declining Pakistan which was struggling to survive in 'desperate times'. Given the circumstances in which the demand for a separate nation called Pakistan arose, she said, even its early secularists had to rely on Islamic terminology to state their case. 'An ambiguous and ample role was awarded to Islam,' she pointed out. Thus, a structural problem with the role of Islam existed in the concept of Pakistan from the very outset. Later, Prime Minister Zulfikar Ali Bhutto flirted with a form of 'folk Islam' to gain popular support while General Zia-ul-Haq openly implemented an 'ulema-inspired, shariatized Islam' and began a process of Islamizing the army. The military, which has been in power for most of that country's life, relies today on a 'Muslim communal discourse' and plays off religious extremism, within and outside the country, against democratic politics to keep itself in command one way or another.

Ayesha Siddiqa, who wrote a fine account of the spread of the Pakistani military's financial tentacles in her book *Military Inc*, warned that jihadist influence was far more widespread than just in the frontier region. Contrary to the belief of many who thought some jihadi groups worked independently from others, she asserted that all jihadists were interconnected. She too pleaded for an attempt by the country's elite to separate Islam from the politics of the state. For that to happen the educated would have to 'create a new narrative' on secular politics and give up attempts to argue that this or that variety of Islam, such as Sufism, could bring moderation to the land.

It is probably too late in the day to introduce any form of secularism in Pakistan. The nation was founded as a separate land for the Muslims of the subcontinent. That did not happen; most Muslims in South Asia live outside Pakistan, which, in fact, stopped further Muslim migration soon after its creation. It has become a military state with a patina of democratic representation without real power, and is becoming a land for ideological Islamists rather than a nation for Muslims.

Secularism, as we have noted, exists in various forms. The French have a hard variety, in which the state tries to preserve a republican non-religious uniformity; the Americans believe in maintaining equidistance from all religions while erecting a wall between religion and the state. India, for its part, offers a diluted variety, in which the secular state attempts to treat all religions equally. The state, as well as the judiciary, often intervene in religious affairs while religious considerations can influence public policy. It nonetheless maintains a pluralist tolerance and allows all religions free play.

Can Pakistan choose the Indian model? Alas, even though the Indian model is only a soft version of secularism, it may not be possible for Pakistan to adopt it. The nation came into being as a homeland for a minority that chose its religious identity as the basis for nationhood. Before long, thanks to cynical manipulation of the polity by civilian as well as military elites, being Muslim alone was not sufficient for a religiously vocal and openly violent section of opinion. A Pakistani citizen should also be a devout member of the global Islamic ummah, insisted extremist mullahs, supported by those who saw the uses of religion in helping them remain in power. Religion came to dominate the public mind, and religious bigots, even though in a minority, captured the commanding heights of opinion. In such a climate, Pakistan's few remaining secularists can merely wave a lonely flag but their position is constantly bludgeoned by vicious religious rhetoric and the threat of violent repercussions.

In contrast to the situation in Pakistan, we could look at Indonesia, the nation with the world's largest Muslim population. That country has also been wracked by terrorist violence and has in recent times had to contend with extremist ideologies that would like to turn society away from its traditional values of tolerant pluralism to an Islamist system of devout orthodoxy. Today, the Indonesian state actively attempts to roll back extremism in thought and practice. Whether it can secure a durable peace is uncertain at this point of time but its intent is to resist extremism. In contrast to Pakistan, Indonesian security forces have continuously battled militant groups, such as the Jemaah Islamiya and its violent splinter groups. Again, in contrast to Pakistan, no section of the official establishment is a sponsor of extremist groups.

Following decades of authoritarian rule, Indonesia became democratic in 1998. Radicals, apparently funded and encouraged in many instances by Saudi sources, seized the freedoms offered by democracy to propagate their intolerant version of Wahhabi Islam. Initially, the state did not pay much attention; then the Bali bombing of 2002 horrified the people and the government moved into action. Importantly, a group of moderate mullahs rallied behind the state and ideologically confronted the militants. Indonesian authorities repeatedly stated their views against Islamic extremism in public. Said Ansad Mbai, Indonesia's counter-terrorism chief, in an interview with *The Washington Post* on 14 May 2010: 'Radical movements cannot be dealt with by only force.' It was necessary, he thought, to uproot an ideology of militancy that turned believers into bombers. 'The good news is that community leaders are willing to oppose radical ideas.' Note that the state in Indonesia is not opposed to religion, but only doing its utmost not to let radical religion take over society.

Is religion our only source of morality and ethics? It is true that over much of history religion has played an immensely important role in helping us create a set of moral and ethical norms for societies and individuals. For example, most religions promote peace on earth as well as fraternity with our fellow human beings. Most religious moral codes, in theory, forbid murder. Most of them encourage charity and help for the poor. Through devotional practices, they suggest self-aware paths to inner calm.

It is also true that secular humanism arose out of religious circumstances, the evolution of European Christianity in particular. The roots of humanistic thought in Europe go back to a Renaissance-era belief that man was made in god's image and therefore should be central to earthly concern. However, secular humanism today rests on a bedrock of reason and is firmly against belief in the supernatural or any faith-based acquisition and propagation of knowledge. To be a secular humanist does not imply you have to be opposed to religious devotion on the basis of personal choice. Many humanists, including several scientists, may be privately religious. But they all agree that the furtherance of human progress against mortal life's adversities must rely on evidentiary observation, proof and a rational ability to either verify or falsify evidence and not on any unquestionable belief system or otherworldly authority.

A basic problem with religious belief is, ironically, one of choice. There are several faiths in the world and faiths within faiths. Which one should you choose as your way to wisdom, bliss, enlightenment or salvation? Each system of unchallengeable faith opposes every other. In the subcontinent, the primary cause of hatred and violence is the fierce struggle between Hindus and Muslims. As I noted, Sikhs and Hindus have had their violent differences, while in Sri Lanka Buddhists and Tamil Hindus have been locked in mortal combat for decades. In Europe, Christians and Muslims have been waging bloody war for centuries. Islamic radicals, who seem to have unforgiving memories, even to this day use the Crusades as a clarion call for revenge against Christians, who they see as continuing that conflict in modern form.

Jews and Christians have for most of their history, since the rise of Christianity, hated one another; it is only in the twentieth century that their conflict has been more or less resolved and scholars of both faiths speak commonly of a Judeo-Christian strain of civilization. That was not the case for the past two millennia; as recently as the mid-twentieth century, a group of European Christians carried out the worst genocide in history against the Jewish people simply because they were Jews. Muslims have also had a difficult relationship with Jews since Prophet Muhammad's era. While in southern Spain there were instances of Muslims protecting Jews from Christian onslaughts, their mutual rhetoric against one another has often been hostile. Today, the Israeli-Palestinian issue has complicated that relationship to such a degree that the communities most hated today by radical Islamists, who would obliterate all non-believers anyway, are three: Jews, Christians and Hindus. Religion hardly promotes peace.

Then there is religion within religion. Catholics and Protestants have for centuries battled one another, apart from fighting Jews and Muslims, in a way that makes Europe's religious history perhaps as bloody as none other. Sunnis and Shias detest each other with a gusto that sometimes surpasses their hatred for the disbelieving kafir. Ahmadiyas in Pakistan are not considered Muslim at all by the majority and are persecuted. In India, caste conflict within the so-called Hindu family is second in intensity only to Hindu-Muslim fights. Even so, every religion, and every sect within each religion, insists that it stands for peace and love for humanity.

Writing in *The New York Times* (24 May 2010), Tenzin Gyatso, the Dalai Lama, made a good case for tolerance among religions. When he was a boy in Tibet, he had presumed that the Buddhist religion must be the best among the world's faiths. 'Now I see how naïve I was and how dangerous the extremes of religious intolerance can be today.' The Dalai Lama discovered the possibility of each religion learning from the others; he realized that there was genuine potential for mutual understanding across faiths. One could preserve faith towards a singular tradition and still respect and appreciate other traditions. Above all, compassion had to be the central message of all religions – compassion for all human beings and not just for those who shared your faith. 'Harmony among the major faiths has become an essential ingredient of peaceful coexistence in our world. From this perspective, mutual understanding among these traditions is not merely the business of religious believers, – it matters for the welfare of humanity as a whole,' he felt.

Alas, given the real intensity of hatred among followers of different religions, the plea of a Nobel Peace Prize winner is likely to end up as just that: a plea full of well-intentioned words while the reality remains starkly different. That is because each faith is structured on a set of unchallengeable assumptions, largely based on arbitrary claims to otherworldly and unproven assertions. The very structure of religious authority depends upon each faith's sanctuary of exclusive distinctiveness, which only the believer can enter.

Well, to each his belief system if anyone wants to choose a faith to follow. Secular tolerance is based on an acceptance of the right to religious freedom. However, religious belief in each specific and competing form is difficult to reconcile with the universal tolerance that secular humanism advocates. For belief is selectively tolerant.

While a secular constitution might make freedom of belief a legal right, no one within a faith has the right to challenge its system of belief. Thus, when Muslims believe that the Koran is in fact Allah's word as conveyed to Prophet Muhammad, no Muslim can have a god-given right to disbelieve that assumption. When a Christian believes that Christ was born to his mother Mary without any sexual activity between his parents, no amount of logical persuasion about biological improbability can move a believer from that conviction. Confrontation happens when followers of Allah's messenger meet head-on with followers of the son of God with competing and un-disprovable belief systems. Religious belief is not refutable by mere earthly logic.

An esoteric discussion of the nature of belief is unnecessary for the purpose of this essay, which is to demonstrate, as clearly as possible, the difficulty posed by each religion based on a set of faith-based paths to knowledge and truth to the exclusion of all others. Although every religion claims the mantle of peace, each one of them carries within itself seeds of exclusivity and, therefore, of potential intolerance.

Religion does not, therefore, exclusively offer humanity a code of ethics or a core of moral values that can make a person a complete individual, as opponents of secularism often insist. It also creates horrifying opportunities for bloodletting, which we might all agree is not exactly a morally fulfilling way of conducting life. It also creates a hierarchy based on unquestionable belief, through which supernatural authority, operating through worldly representatives, stifles inquiry and thus closes avenues of a necessary advancement of human civilization towards a better world.

Secular humanism and its appropriate vehicle, liberal democracy, on the other hand, open up routes to free inquiry. They enable us to pursue knowledge – verifiable, evidence-based understanding – in a manner that is open to dissent and challenge. Scientific inquiry would not have been possible without this revolution in reason, which occurred with the separation of religious authority from political power.

Prior to that epochal development in the story of humanity, real curiosity about the nature of existence could only get some play in speculative philosophy; those who questioned fundamental assumptions, such as Galileo, often perished at the stake, or, at any rate, were condemned by religious overlords directing, supposedly on divine authority, the destiny of humankind. If it was the papacy in Europe, it was Brahminism in caste-splintered India, and the ulema across the Islamic world. Through much of history, it was trade and exchange of information that led to advancement of knowledge. However, the speed with which history gathered momentum after the victory of secular reason over the power of faith phenomenally lifted the quality of human existence.

The world today is, notwithstanding undoubted shortcomings, a better place to inhabit thanks to open inquiry, and not faith, though religion, we should acknowledge, played a comprehensive and significant role in human development until the rise of secular reason, scientific discovery and the spirit of liberal tolerance. It continues to play a central role in the lives of most people across the world today.

In 1791, the newly minted American Constitution offered several innovative features through a Bill of Rights. Two were especially crucial for the subsequent expansion of liberal democracy. One, as we have mentioned, was creating separate spaces for religion and state; the other was to guarantee freedom of the press, which meant ensuring freedom of expression for all citizens. Today, these form twin pillars in several modern constitutions to uphold liberal, pluralist, tolerant democracy.

As we can agree, secular liberalism implies freedom of speech, free inquiry and free opinionating as well as freedom of religious expression. A religion, after all, is an opinion and must accordingly enjoy protection in any liberal democracy. Most formally religious societies, however, do not grant the same courtesy to secular reason or, for that matter, to any religion other than the official creed. For example, in a fundamentally religious nation like Saudi Arabia, blasphemy laws ensure that free pursuit of any religion other than the state's version of Islam is impossible. In Egypt, a group of Islamic lawyers recently demanded an official ban on the *Arabian Nights*, that centuries-old collection of folk tales, on the ground that it was obscene. A spokesman of the group told the TV station Al Arabiya, 'I was shocked at the offensive phrases it contains,' and proceeded to list references to sex in the book as 'calls to sin'. The Egyptian Writers' Union stepped in to call the lawyers as bad as the Taliban, who had destroyed sculptures of the Buddha in Bamiyan, Afghanistan.

Freedom of expression remains a crucial component of liberal democracy, as does religion as a point of view. That is why a democracy such as India's gives all of us freedom, under Article 25 of the Constitution, to pursue religion as a fundamental right. For those who might choose to be non-religious or anti-religious, the right to remain so is guaranteed by the primary right to freedom of expression as well as the freedom to pursue whichever belief system we might wish to, including atheism, which after all is a viewpoint that denies the existence of any divine entity and thus represents a position against religion. These two fundamental rights are two sides of the same coin. We must protect both if we wish to uphold liberal democracy.

Writing in the 1830s while travelling across America, the Frenchman Alexis de Tocqueville was perhaps the first major political thinker to notice what was then a new phenomenon in democratic society. It was the concept of a free press as the primary vehicle of free expression. Democracy itself was a new development, limited at the time in spread and depth. Freedom of the press had, however, for the first time been enshrined in a written constitution just four decades before Tocqueville arrived to study the working of American democracy. He recognized immediately the vital importance of the press and wrote about it in *Democracy In America:*

> It causes political life to circulate through all the parts of that vast territory. Its eye is constantly open to detect the secret springs of political designs and to summon the leaders of all parties to the bar of public opinion. It rallies the interest of the community round certain principles and draws up the creed of every party; for it affords a means of intercourse between those who hear and address each other without ever coming into immediate contact.

He underscored the crucial role of a free press when he asserted, 'To suppose that they (newspapers) only serve to protect freedom would be to diminish their importance: they maintain civilization.'

The idea of a free press, and therefore of freedom of expression, is a quintessentially modern idea. It grew initially out of the needs of expanding international trade and its concomitant need for ever-expanding information. It later became, as Tocqueville observed, the vital vehicle for exchange and trade of public opinion, so central to the functioning of democracy. Today, the existence or absence of freedom of expression marks a point that distinguishes a free democracy from an authoritarian regime. Indeed, the notion of free expression and inquiry could not exist in religion-dominated societies, in which ecclesiastical authority determined what was true or desirable for the public.

Tocqueville realized that religion and democracy posed problems for each other. The dynamics of democracy, that free spirit of inquiry and speech, undermined religious otherworldliness. All religions lay claim to eternal truth, and to maintain that claim, every religion has to maintain its particular brand of dogma, without which it would forfeit its claim to exclusive wisdom. Yet democracy, by encouraging individualism and material progress, inclined citizens to be averse to dogmatic beliefs. This apparent paradox, Tocqueville thought, was best resolved by allowing the state and religion to thrive separately. While the former would boost the pursuit of material happiness, the latter would promote restraint.

Perhaps the spirit of the age he was writing in and the deep religiosity of the society he was writing about drew Tocqueville to such a practical compromise. Secularism and religion, however, each with its own set of ethics, coincide at several spots.

Humans aspire to improving life's conditions. Without that spirit of aspiration, neither fire nor agriculture would have been invented, nor would the age of reason have come about to lay a foundation for modern growth, prosperity and longer lives.

All human life has, therefore, a view of the future. Democratic societies, by liberating people's minds from dogmatic strictures and allowing the flowering of a spirit of inquiry, support an especially dynamic interpretation of futuristic aspiration. Most religions also have a vision for the future. The difference is that religion generally offers a vision of the future beyond life on earth, whether through the possibility of life in paradise, or in hell, or through reincarnation, or through the promise of nirvana after a recycle of birth and death, or through a variety of otherworldly expectations. Secular democracy, on the other hand, by promoting progress, aspires to improve life in the here and now regardless of what might or might not happen in afterlife.

A binding ethic of most religions is delayed gratification. That ethic defines many of the mores that religion stipulates for society, including a sense of restraint, a spirit of benevolence and cooperation with fellow humans, and an appeal that aggression in its various forms be tamed. As I have argued, those ethics generally apply to adherents of each faith, almost invariably by excluding followers of other faiths.

While religion can and does provide a system of ethics and morality, the secular sphere can and does generate a parallel code of ethics to make liberal democracy work. The founding basis for that code is the constitution, which lays out dos and don'ts for a democratic citizenry. Thus, a stricture like 'thou shall not kill' is laid out in the form of laws against murder, the violation of which will lead to severe consequences in the here and now and not in some mythical afterlife. Similarly, if religion asks us to love and respect other human beings, a constitution, such as India's, by asking for secular tolerance and pluralism, more or less promotes the same sentiment. The only difference is that tolerance is universal, regardless of faith, and is not restricted, as most religions effectively are, to any particular band of believers.

The argument that secular reason has no internal coherence, and is just as valid or invalid as religion is in humankind's search for truth, is little more than academic sophistry. It has little relevance to the way human history has actually unfolded and has had zero impact on daily life outside sociology departments in universities. To engage in a detailed refutation of such arguments is unnecessary for the purpose of this essay and would amount to avoidable indulgence in intellectual callisthenics.

As for those who argue that secular reason has not been able to reduce violence in the world, it is gratifying that critics of secularism are ready to acknowledge, however implicitly, that religion has had a comparatively bloody history. Secular reason makes no claim that it has an answer to human hatred apart from offering an appeal to rational discourse that might provide civilized alternatives to violence. It is true that some anti-church revolutionaries during the French Revolution, Robespierre and Saint-Just, for instance, were murderous in their attitude towards clerics and executed some. They were, however, hardly tolerant liberals in those dark hours of the dawn of democracy.

Indeed, some secular societies in modern times have been among the worst in history in their levels and intensity of violence. Josef Stalin's Soviet Union, Mao Zedong's China, and Pol Pot's Kampuchea were secular states that had banned religion. Millions perished under their tyranny. Adolf Hitler's Germany was a secular socialist nation, yet it massacred Jews and other minorities. North Korea's ruler, the ridiculous Kim Jong Il, has built a near-divine aura around himself and his late father Kim Il Sung; the people have to endure famine while they worship the great leader.

The point is that those societies can be called secular only in declared intent. In reality they are just nominally different from religious dictatorships. The cult of personality worship in such societies is as intense, and the throttling of reasoned debate as harsh, as in any god-fearing society of the past. They cannot be called secular, liberal democracies, where tolerance of diversity is a norm or where differences of opinion have formal outlets, like houses of parliament and a free press, or where a liberal constitution guarantees freedoms and a judiciary guards the freedoms as best as it can.

That is why it is important to accept that any secular polity that wants to promote pluralism must first provide a liberal constitutional framework as well as a social environment that facilitates tolerance. In a multi-religious, multicultural, multiethnic, multilingual nation such as India, tolerance is not just a desirable social goal but a necessity for preserving the idea of India. Diversity of religion or ethnicity must not merely be tolerated; it must be celebrated in a nation like ours. We have no choice. We must find ways to expand the liberal space on our political-ideological spectrum in order to sustain this unique democratic national experiment we call India. Without a secular-liberal spirit as the vehicle of pluralist tolerance, democracy loses depth even as it expands, thus degenerating steadily beyond recognition.

Ten

SEEKING LIBERAL DEMOCRACY

Not all democracies are liberal from their inception; at least not in the way we now understand liberal democracy. The founding fathers of the US wrote a classically liberal constitution, one that serves as a model for many other aspiring democracies, yet the nation waited over a century and a half – until 1964-65 – before it became a liberal democracy in the full sense of the term. It was only then that the US could rightfully claim that all its adult citizens could freely vote and would not be discriminated against on the basis of race, ethnicity or gender. From the time it was founded as a democratic republic in the late eighteenth century till the first half of the twentieth, discrimination was rampant in much of the US, ranging from the obvious, like slavery and segregation, to the relatively trivial. In the nineteenth century, for example, some American cities disallowed public appearances by 'unsightly' persons. In Chicago, 'any person who is diseased, maimed, mutilated, or in any way deformed, so as to be an unsightly or disgusting subject', was not allowed to come into public view 'under the penalty of a fine of $1 for each offense'. This in a society which today is perhaps the most user-friendly of all for handicapped or maimed persons, where discrimination on the basis of 'unsightly' appearance can carry fines far in excess of one dollar. The change did not happen on autopilot; it required leadership.

America's journey from there to here was neither easy nor painless. Its citizens fought a fierce civil war over the issue of slavery and states' rights in which over 600,000 people died. America produced enlightened leaders, from presidents and pastors to legislators and judges, who changed laws and mindsets. They struggled against powerful interests and deep-seated prejudice. They established a public school system, which tried to instil in children a sense of tolerance while keeping the arena of public education and legislation strictly secular in line with the constitution. At the same time, religion did not disappear or lose influence over the masses. Americans remained overwhelmingly religious, with a huge majority of them telling opinion pollsters as late as the early twenty-first century that they visited churches and synagogues, mosques and temples regularly. In America, secularism means the state is indifferent to religion, not anti-religion.

Liberalism demands that all opinions have space to be expressed in a democracy. As religion is a world-view, an opinion, it too should have space for expression just like political or artistic opinion. Also, as various religions have different world-views, every religion should have the right to free expression in a democracy aspiring to be liberal. The state by implementing its constitution must provide that space and ensure that all opinion is expressed, or opposed, within the confines of law and without violence. If a state is unable to provide and sustain that liberal framework so essential to free speech, a process of democratic decay may set in. Democracy is after all like a living organism; it must be nurtured to help it thrive and survive.

Fareed Zakaria cautioned against the rise of what he described as 'illiberal democracies'. In an essay in *Foreign Affairs* in 1997, and later in a book *The Future of Freedom: Illiberal Democracy at Home and Abroad*, he drew attention to a disturbing phenomenon, which was the rise of democratically elected regimes that routinely deprived their citizens of basic rights and freedoms. Democracy in modern times has been taken to mean liberal democracy, that is, a political system marked by free and fair elections as well as by constitutional liberalism: the rule of law, a separation of powers, and the protection of liberties of speech, assembly, religion, and property. However, Zakaria feels that while democracy seems to be spreading in the world, liberalism is not.

Free and fair elections are doubtless a basic condition of democracy. If accompanied by a minimum degree of free speech and assembly, free elections mark out a nation as democratic. Constitutional liberalism, however, is not primarily about how a nation selects its government. It seeks to protect an individual's autonomy and dignity against coercion by the state, church and society, and it developed as a system in the West to defend an individual's right to life and property, freedom of speech and religion. By the 1840s, most Western countries had largely acquired aspects of liberalism, but were not full-fledged democracies.

In much of the rest of the world in the twentieth century, emerging nations were autocracies of one shade or another, some starting out as democracies that soon turned authoritarian. Many later moved gradually towards 'liberalizing autocracy', or in some cases towards 'liberalizing semi-democracy'; a single party or a patriarchal figure controlled the state, though in some nations they went through a charade of elections that merely consolidated their hold on power. In East Asia, a form of constitutional liberalism, starting with economic liberalization, took hold but electoral democracy did not, until much later. In Africa, democratization was rapid with little sign of expanding constitutional liberalism. In Central Asia, elections have led to the ascent to power of authoritarian rulers, weak legislatures and judiciaries, with virtually no corresponding spread of civil liberties. In the Islamic world, elections have in many nations created an increased role for theocratic politics, eroding traditions of secularism and tolerance, Zakaria points out.

In brief, Zakaria's argument is that even though there are no respectable options to democracy, problems of governance remain within illiberal democracies. 'Illiberal democracies gain legitimacy, and thus strength,' he writes, 'from the fact that they are reasonably democratic.' Conversely, he adds, the greatest danger that illiberal democracy poses, other than to its own people, is that it will discredit liberal democracy itself, casting a shadow over democratic governance. Every wave of democracy, he continues, has been followed by setbacks in which the system was seen as inadequate and new alternatives were sought by ambitious leaders and restless masses... Democracy without constitutional liberalism, he concludes, is not simply inadequate, but dangerous, bringing with it the erosion of liberty, the abuse of power, ethnic divisions, and even war.

To summarize his thesis, constitutional liberalism is distinct from democracy. Democracy may be flourishing but liberalism is not. It may be time for supporters of democracy to assist the consolidation of liberalism rather than the expansion of electoral democracy. Democracy can degenerate without liberalism, and 'liberal autocracies' are preferable to illiberal democracies for development and prosperity.

In India's case, we have a republic that is democratic and constitutionally liberal from the very outset. The question is: can it lose the liberal spirit that is outlined splendidly in its Constitution to the extent that it becomes an illiberal democracy? To answer, we might consider two issues raised by Zakaria's thesis: First, is democracy a hindrance to growth and development? Second, any people can declare their nation to be democratic but can they maintain it without inculcating a liberal character? How then does a democracy become liberal or, in India's case, remain liberal?

The word liberal in this context does not refer to who rules in a democracy but how that rule is exercised. The government should have limited powers and checks and balances must exist to its exercise of authority. In a liberal democracy, power is limited by the rule of law, usually as spelt out in a constitution, but ultimately by individual rights. As Marc Plattner, co-editor of the *Journal of Democracy* and a leading thinker on democratic theory and practice, asserts in an article he wrote in *Foreign Affairs*: 'The idea of natural or inalienable rights, which today are most commonly called "human rights", originated with liberalism.' The primacy of individual rights, he added, meant that the protection of the private sphere, along with plurality and diversity of ends that people sought in their pursuit of happiness, was a key element of a liberal political order.

Further, the political doctrine at the source of liberalism contains an egalitarian and majoritarian dimension; it implies that all legitimate power is derived from the consent of individuals, who are by nature not only free but are equal. No one has a natural claim to rule over another.

Individual rights form the core of any liberal order. Conversely, without individual rights guaranteed by a liberal constitution, upheld by an independent judiciary, a robust legislature and an executive with limited powers, we cannot call any system 'liberal'.

By definition, there can be no such entity as a 'liberal autocracy'. The examples Zakaria cites, the British colony of Hong Kong or Lee Kwan Yew's Singapore, as instances of successful liberal autocracies, were in fact not liberal at all. They were benevolent autocracies; they lacked most of the essential qualities of a liberal order apart from enforcing the rule of law without any concomitant restraint on executive power. Importantly, they did not value the centrality of the rights of the individual; on the contrary, Lee Kwan Yew argued for Confucian harmony at the expense of individual rights, for 'Asian values' as opposed to Western liberal individualism.

Zakaria appears to side with those who, like Lee, believe that a wise and far-sighted, and therefore benevolent, autocracy is a better vehicle for rapid development than democracy can ever be for a traditional society. The problem is how to ensure the necessary benevolence without which any such choice might be a losing gamble. The question is relevant for us Indians at a time when many of our middle-class and upper-class compatriots are getting impatient with democratic sloth and looking enviously at China's authoritarian model as a better prospect for the achievement of rapid growth. In fact, as several studies have shown, the growth rates of democracies have not been noticeably worse than those of authoritarian regimes. Besides, the success of some of the East Asian economies may have a lot to do with their rapid transition to an export-oriented trade strategy which helped them profit from the huge growth in the world economy in the 1960s. They seem to have taken a cue from Japan, which pursued a similar approach. Add to that the fact that they all had fairly high rates of literacy. These are all choices that can be made in a democracy through discussion, as indeed they are in many democracies, with positive results. The difference in an autocracy would be the lack of popular and transparent debate or discussion, which admittedly can sometimes be a trying process, but that does not suggest any inherent superiority of an autocracy over a democracy when it comes to making policy choices for growth.

The developmental achievements of the East Asian economies Zakaria cites have doubtless been spectacular over a relatively short period of time. However, the record of authoritarian rule around the world is far spottier. In Africa, for example, dictators have destroyed the economic prospects of so many nations. Even an oil-rich economy like Nigeria has not benefited from authoritarian rule. Zimbabwe is a disaster. Democratic South Africa, on the other hand, has had relative stability with growth.

China, which some Indians have begun to cite as a developmental model to emulate, is an interesting example of how uncertain the gamble on benevolent rule can be. In 1978, the authoritarian ruler, Deng Xiaoping, overturned the central developmental principles espoused by another authoritarian potentate, Mao Zedong, and unleashed a growth story that had little to do with communism in nominally communist China.

The relatively benevolent Deng's return to power – he had been reviled and ousted by Mao during the Cultural Revolution – and rise after the death of the whimsically inclined Mao was hardly foreseeable at the time. That he would launch the Four Modernizations initiative in 1978 to clear the runway for China's stunning economic take-off was even less predictable. Yet it happened and it worked. Under Mao's disastrous socialist engineering experiments – the Great Leap Forward, the Cultural Revolution – millions perished while the economy limped along. China's capitalist growth under communist watch was a version of Singapore massively magnified by authoritarian party rule. An authoritarian regime liberalized the economy in critical ways to release a tide of market forces that swept away decades of socialist stagnation, all the while keeping its hard fist on a lid to shut out popular political aspirations. Deng's benevolence was only for economic reform. When it came to demands for liberalization of the polity, Deng ruthlessly cracked the whip. China grew rapidly under autocratic rule, plain and simple; it is not a liberal autocracy.

Some contrast China's sequencing of policy preferences with that of Russia in the 1980s. In the final years of the Soviet Union, Mikhail Gorbachov pushed 'glasnost', or openness, more rapidly than 'perestroika', or restructuring reform. In China, Deng chose the opposite. He opted for economic reform and firmly kept openness at bay. In other words, Gorbachov opted for political democratization first whereas Deng preferred launching economic liberalization while retaining autocratic control.

China's spectacular economic success and Russia's relative lack of it in the 1990s might suggest the wisdom of Deng's sequencing over Gorbachov's. The political, historical and cultural circumstances of the two countries were, however, quite different and scholars of development are still debating the post-communist sequencing issue. Some say that China's Confucian culture, with its emphasis on harmony and hierarchical order, facilitated consensus building and may account for Deng's success. Russia, shattered by decades of Stalinist oppression, had a more difficult social terrain for achievement of the basic consensus necessary for stable growth. This indicates that a sudden introduction of democracy in certain social and political circumstances may not be appropriate, but it does not confirm any general trend.

In India's case, all such arguments are perhaps moot. It is difficult to imagine this extraordinary adventure in post-colonial nation building to be in any framework other than a democratic one. Given the tremendous variety of language, ethnicity, race and religion prevalent in the emerging nation, India's founding fathers wisely opted for outright democracy over any sequenced detour through benevolent autocracy.

Today, India's economy continues to grow at a pace that is second only to China's among the world's larger economies. It was economic policy choices made in the 1950s that held back the pace of growth and consequently, the rate at which poverty could be reduced and the middle class expanded. Again, it was a deliberate, and democratic, change of policy that led to a significant liberalization of the economy in 1991, when the nation faced a balance of payments crisis, which put the economy on a fast track, though signs of change had become evident in the 1980s. The reforms that have so far been carried out are by no means adequate but they are significant. Since 2003, India's economy has expanded at a rate that has been almost continuously above 7 per cent annually, with a dip below that during the global financial crisis that hit everyone in 2008. In contrast to the first four decades of virtual stagnation, in the course of the last decade and a half the middle class has expanded impressively and the proportion of people living below the line of absolute poverty has declined. Poverty remains a stark fact of Indian life, but it is less than it was.

The decline in poverty should perhaps have been more rapid and the growth faster. An initial widening of the income gap between the richer sections of society and the poorer ones is also an outcome of more rapid growth because, first, the better-off have more investible savings and are accordingly better placed to increase their wealth; and, second, the already relatively better-off are more educated and thus in a better position to seize the fruits of economic growth and innovation than the uneducated poor. Overall, however, India is visibly more prosperous than it was twenty years ago. Per capita income and longevity are both rising faster than they did during the decades of central planning.

Economic advancement and development, therefore, are at least as likely to succeed or fail in a democratic framework as in an autocratic one. Making the right policy choices, and building a popular consensus over the approach selected, might even be considered a better way of generating long-term growth and prosperity than autocratic arbitrariness. Globally, the growth rates of the economies of democratic nations have not been noticeably inferior to those of undemocratic regimes.

Nevertheless, the other question raised by Zakaria's thoughtful thesis is a difficult one to answer. Any nation can declare itself to be democratic by going through the motion of holding elections, but will that alone make it a liberal democracy? Alternatively, should it be correctly called an electoral democracy when it is only partly free? Also, importantly for India, can a democracy, which starts out with proclaimed liberal intentions, sustain its accommodative character in a traditional sociocultural milieu that is unfavourable to liberalism? The Indian Constitution is unambiguously liberal in intent, but are India's sociocultural conditions suited to liberalism? Was India ripe for liberal democracy? Can India, after sixty years, still be called liberal or has a distance grown between the spirit of the Constitution and reality? These are indeed issues of grave concern for India's future.

Clearly, India's survival as a functioning democracy has confounded its critics. Elections are held regularly, governments at both the federal and state levels are frequently changed, civil society groups proliferate, the courts are independent as is, by and large, the press. The very presence of these features does not, however, add up to a liberal democracy, though they form key elements of any democratic polity.

Where the liberal quotient of India's sociopolitical structure may be under threat, and therefore could become a threat one day to its continuance as a genuine, viable democracy, is the quality of its performance in three areas. The first is weakening governance in terms of the state's ability to enforce as well as abide by the rule of law; the second is a related area of poor accountability, principally the result of an overwhelmed and underperforming judiciary as well as a poorly informed public that still suffers from high illiteracy; and the third is a growing intolerance, evident in the current trend of religious, regional and cultural animosities that I discussed earlier but also in the tendency of a few groups to foment intolerant tactics for the redressal of real and imagined grievances, bypassing the democratic route offered by the Constitution, which they berate as an impotent document.

The act of electing a nation's rulers freely and fairly entails protection of basic rights such as freedom of speech, assembly and association. In that sense, India is much more than an electoral democracy. But the ability of the Indian state to implement policies is weak and, to all appearances, is becoming weaker by the day. Whether it is collection of taxes, or public education, or public health and hygiene, or power and water supply, or police supervision, the state seems to come up short in several key areas of public service. This despite a booming economy, elite educational institutions, – such as the Indian Institutes of Technology and Indian Institutes of Management, to say nothing of a few fine medical colleges and research institutions – as well as highly skilled engineers and technicians, a combination of skills and intellect that should have been able to control the deterioration in public services given the right incentives, investment and leadership. But it hasn't worked: public services continue to stagnate.

As it happens, the quality of life may be among the world's poorest for many but it is not bad for India's elite. Perhaps attitudes inherited from a traditional upper-caste-dominated social hierarchy allow people to accept blatant inequality and unfairness, but those who occupy the higher tiers of society – industrialists and top executives, senior bureaucrats and politicians, media owners and celebrity journalists – lead a very comfortable existence. So long as you have either money to buy your way or the right connections you can lead a life that compares favourably to life in advanced societies.

The trouble is that those involved in policy making or implementation are rarely confronted with the harshness of daily life. Their world is in a way sealed off from the rest of the people. The stark difference is visible in, say, what is called Lutyen's Delhi, that tree-lined central part of the city where many government decision makers live. They have few water or power shortages; if the electricity goes off on a rare occasion, the spacious, well-tended and well-guarded bungalows in central New Delhi have generators that step in to continue power supply. Meanwhile, the standard of public services – water and power supply, public hospitals, public hygiene, street conditions, recreational facilities – in all cities continue to decline, making living conditions in urban agglomerations in India rank among the worst in the world.

Ever since the economic liberalization of 1991, the private sector in India has come into play in meaningful ways, and both productivity and innovation have risen. India's recent performance in the economic sphere has been impressive. For efficient functioning, however, markets need a system of peaceful resolution of disputes and delivery of contracts. India's judicial system remains way behind those vital needs of an expanding liberalized economy.

The reason I mentioned failing public services is that poor governance in a democracy is generally the consequence of weak accountability. To help maintain a liberal legal and administrative framework, in which people are encouraged and infused with confidence in seeking legal remedies rather than bypassing the law or taking the law into their hands, thus opening enabling avenues for violence and intolerance, public accountability must be an essential element of governance. Good governance rests on the twin pillars of transparency and accountability. While transparency of the Indian state's functioning has improved with the enactment of a right to information law, public accountability remains poor. This, in my view, is because of the weak performance of two arms of governance, the judiciary and the police.

The Indian judicial system probably holds a world record for tardiness in meting out justice. Indian courts are clogged with over thirty million cases, the number rising by the day, with cases lying with the Supreme Court alone rising to 84,000 in early 2010. In 1984, India had ten judges for every one million persons; by 2007, that ratio had declined to six judges per million, according to the Law Commission. Even Bangladesh has a better ratio of twelve per million. Many cases, especially in the lower courts, are frivolous and should have been disposed of long ago. Justice, however, grinds its way at a lethargic pace. Adjournments of hearings are granted at the slightest excuse, cases are repeatedly postponed, and suspicions of corruption have begun to mount. From lower courts to high courts, tales are legion of bribes having to be paid to minor officials just to have cases brought to the attention of the bench.

Visiting an Indian court for a hearing can be a nightmarish experience. Therefore, the incentive to seek justice through the legal system is often weighed by citizens against doing so through other means. In numerous disputes over property, for example, cases drag on for over two decades, exhausting the patience of the litigants and discouraging other aspirants to justice from filing cases. Along the way, property rights get devalued in people's minds, thus damaging a singularly important element in the functioning of market forces. Again, the number of cases in the courts involving bounced cheques alone is nearly four million. What could prevent people, in the circumstances, from indulging in fraudulent activities that hamper business transactions and lower trust in society? Worse, banks and credit card organizations themselves have been often known to employ extralegal, strong-armed methods to recover loans because going to court would be fruitless.

To be fair, the law ministry has lately woken up to the problem. It is, however, a gigantic task that the ministry and judicial leaders have to undertake. From building infrastructure across the country in order to house hundreds of additional courts to appointing and training thousands of judges and administrative officials, it is a task that is likely to take at least half a century to bring the system on par with the courts of developed democracies. Till then, assuming matters do not deteriorate, as is quite likely, public accountability through the judicial system will remain poor, with unfortunate consequences for the peaceful and legal resolution of disputes. With avenues to legal remedies choked as they are, people will increasingly want to take the law into their hands even as rising expectations continue to fuel impatience.

As for the police, India's police to population ratio is just 126 per 100,000 persons, which is around half that recommended by the United Nations for peacetime policing. India's policemen have to deal with terrible working conditions over long hours for extremely poor pay. They live in filthy accommodation and often do not have the equipment they need for policing. Naturally, the tendency to cut corners is high.

The police force operates on the basis of the nineteenth-century Police Act, modelled by British rulers after another security force they had devised in order to suppress people yearning for freedom, the Royal Irish Constabulary. And the ruler versus ruled quotient of police relations with the people has not changed since then. It is important for us to understand the nature and style of imperial rule. British administrative officers, numbering barely a thousand over the entire territory comprising present-day India, Pakistan and Bangladesh, ruled their subjects through a set of elite services, chief among which were the Indian Civil Service and the Imperial Police. Natives filled the subordinate ranks and were isolated from the officers. The ranks were told under the Police Act to 'obey all orders lawfully given by the officers', and a range of pomp and pageantry was devised to reinforce the authority of the rulers. The poorly paid and little-trained subordinates were the points of contact with the people, with the administrators of the ICS and IP maintaining an exalted and deliberate distance from the masses to increase their aura. Direct recruitment into the police officers' ranks was closed for Indians till 1921, and even after that date the number of Indian officers remained disproportionately low.

Writes Arvind Verma, an expert on criminal justice at Indiana University, in *The State of India's Democracy*: 'The citizens endured daily humiliations and oppression from the bureaucracy. The only relief from the marauding army of government servants came from the senior officers who alone could control and discipline them. Yet the aura of senior officers was such that no citizen dared to approach them.' Verma adds that while the British, through their inspections and administrative mechanisms, would occasionally punish a corrupt officer, they insulated themselves and only in rare cases took action.

Regrettably, the situation today is not very different. In independent India, the Indian Administrative Service, which succeeded the ICS, and the Indian Police Service continue as the principal arms of state administration. In style and attitude, members of the two services remain beholden to the imperial tradition while the masses of ordinary people still treat them as their rulers.

In 1950, India's new rulers strengthened the coercive powers of the police system. Jawaharlal Nehru's government enacted a Preventive Detention Act, which allowed the state to imprison anyone suspected of posing a threat to society. India thus became the first democratic country to enact a prevention provision of this kind. Since then several laws have been passed by the Union government, under the supervision of parties of the left and the right, to strengthen the provision of preventive detention. During the 1975-77 Emergency rule of Indira Gandhi, when civil liberties had been in any case suspended, almost 100,000 supporters and suspected sympathizers of the Opposition, including journalists and civil society activists, were arrested under the Maintenance of Internal Security Act (MISA), which had been enacted to deal with anti-national persons and foreign saboteurs.

Today, thousands languish without trial in jails across India. Several have spent more time in jail than the periods of imprisonment their alleged crimes would have attracted in a court of law. Many have been arrested under preventive detention laws. The police have been given extraordinary powers of search, seizure and preventive detention. Under sections 41 to 56 of the Criminal Procedure Code (CrPC), a police officer may arrest any citizen without a warrant authorized by a magistrate. Section 54 authorizes a police officer to arrest a person against whom he has 'reasonable suspicion' of having committed a crime. What reasonable suspicion might be is said to 'depend upon circumstances of the particular case'. No formal complaint from a citizen is necessary for the police to arrest anyone under this rule.

In many cases, the court trials drag on and on while the accused suffer imprisonment for years in dehumanizing conditions. Human rights are routinely violated and torture of prisoners is common. Custodial deaths happen while complaints thrive of fake encounters in which the police get rid of suspects. The 2002-03 report of the National Human Rights Commission said 183 persons died while in police custody that year; the commission had also received complaints that year of eighty-three staged encounters in which the police were alleged to have eliminated suspects.

In dealing with armed rebellions, such as in Kashmir and Punjab, the police and paramilitary forces have had to take extraordinary measures to protect the nation as well as themselves. Preventive laws have had to be applied in specific sectors with some justification. However, so many instances of fake encounters have occurred in these states that the National Human Rights Commission has had to advise the state governments involved to investigate all complaints and report back to it. Blatant violations of human rights weaken respect for the law and tarnish democracy.

The problem is that such reckless behaviour by the guardians of law and order does not help the cause of enforcing the rule of law in a nation where, as it is, poor education has not helped prepare the base for a social consensus on civic responsibilities. Any system of order in a democratic society to be governed by a system of law has to have a minimum level of consensual agreement on all sides – a social contract, if you will – on the need for the rule of law as well as a general recognition of civic duties and responsibilities. If the enforcers of law violate citizens' legal rights, and citizens on their part look upon the enforcers as malevolent oppressors rather than benevolent protectors, the result is what India suffers today in chaotic abundance.

Organized crime flourishes, citizens flout the law with impunity, and rebellion sprouts shoots. From the law of the jungle ruling traffic and threatening safety in cities, through brazen flouting of the law by land mafias, through tyranny of landlords and caste gangs in villages, to armed rebellion sweeping through swathes of the nation, the scope of sustaining tolerance in a democratic environment seems to be eroding. Without that liberal tolerance, however, the idea of India dies.

In previous chapters I discussed disruptive intolerance principally in the religious-cultural context because that is where the threat to the concept of a pluralist, liberal India is most visible. It is also the kind of intolerance that marked the bloody birth of the nation and has remained with us as a nagging, and frequently searing, pain. Lately, however, a type of armed and violent intolerance has begun to haunt the nation; a threat that Prime Minister Manmohan Singh in 2006 called 'the single biggest internal security challenge' ever. The Maoist movement in central India threatens to tear the country asunder in the name of securing justice for the poor.

The Maoist movement began in 1967 in a remote village of north Bengal called Naxalbari. The Naxalites, as they came to be called, were a breakaway faction of the Communist Party of India (Marxist). Their violent encounters in the 1960s and early 1970s were as often with cadres and supporters of the CPI(M) as with the police and landowners in West Bengal, Bihar and the north-eastern part of Andhra Pradesh. The movement, wracked by factional fights and a futile attempt to spread their violent tactics to major cities like Kolkata, died out by the mid-1970s and did not seriously threaten again until the early twenty-first century. Today, intelligence analysts believe the Naxalites are developing the capacity to split India right through the middle in an arc stretching from Nepal to Andhra Pradesh.

In 2004, two Naxalite groups, the Maoist Communist Centre and the Communist Party of India (Marxist-Leninist) People's War, merged to form the Communist Party of India (Maoist), which had the stated goal of overthrowing the

Indian government. Going by official estimates, they have 40,000 permanent cadres and around 100,000 members of an armed militia. The Union home ministry believes 223 out of India's 604 districts are affected by Maoist activities. They have established 'people's courts' and a revenue collection system. As the war with the police rages, the unfortunate people of the affected areas are caught between meeting the extortion demands of the Maoists and the searching interrogations of a strong-armed police force. From operating predominantly in rural, hilly and forested areas among tribal populations, the Maoists are now moving into urban areas in the affected states. This has helped them raise more money.

They have mastered ways of raising funds to finance their rebellion. By the home ministry's estimate, Maoists extort Rs 1,500 crores every year by threatening violence. They obtain pay-offs from businesses, contractors, truck operators, landowners, mining corporations and the police stations they raid. Apart from straightforward kidnapping, looting and robbing, they extract taxes from people living in areas they have under their control. They make money from charges on poppy cultivation. The rebellion churns out its own funds to buy armaments and pay salaries to cadres. By all accounts, they run an efficient, self-financed economy.

At the time of writing, in the states of Jharkhand, Chhattisgarh, and parts of Orissa and West Bengal, the Maoists have chunks of territory under their control. Their war with the police continues unabated, resulting in rampant death and destruction. While Andhra Pradesh waged a successful campaign against the Maoists, combining aggressive policing with targeted development and public affairs initiatives, the governments of the other affected areas have so far been largely unsuccessful in countering the violent rebellion.

Meanwhile, as the Union government contemplates whether to use the military to subdue the Maoists in their so-called Red Corridor running through east-central India, sympathetic intellectuals defend the rebellion in the salons, magazines and television studios of Delhi and Mumbai. That is exactly how it should be in a democracy, where various contesting viewpoints ought to have legitimate outlets in public forums, even when some of these intellectuals bash the system that allows them to express support for a movement that aims at destroying pluralist tolerance and democracy.

The novelist Arundhati Roy is prominent among such intellectuals, and her views have wide, international reach. She employs that reach to portray the Indian state as a merciless oppressor and the Maoists as victimized champions of the poor. In a talk she gave in New York to a left-wing audience in March 2010, she referred to India as a 'fake democracy', even though the kind of contrarian views she holds would only be allowed free expression and wide circulation in a democracy such as India, with all its undoubtedly illiberal shortcomings, and would never have been allowed in the society that the Maoists hold up as their model, the brutal regime of Mao's China.

In an interview on CNN-IBN, journalist Karan Thapar asked Roy: 'So the state of India's dispossessed and poor is proof that Indian democracy has failed?'

'It's proving that there is a structural violence,' replied Roy. 'Mahasweta Devi (a renowned, award-winning Bengali novelist) a few years ago in Frankfurt described Indian democracy as a tapestry with parts of it as silken and parts of it as tattered but it all holds together. Now what has happened is that the silken parts have sequined and the tattered parts are torn and the poor are falling in. And the Indian state is following them with guns, with helicopter gunships. We are in crisis.'

It is difficult to argue with extreme views couched in elegant metaphors. Roy has easy access to a range of forums, particularly television, because she is a famous author living in a functioning democracy. She can say what she likes and she does not hesitate to do so. We listen to her carefully; some of us agree and some, I suspect a substantial majority, don't. We don't want her books to be banned even when we find her assertions outrageous. Indian democracy still works, warts and all.

Mahasweta Devi was quite correct in saying what she did in Frankfurt. Indian democracy is indeed a tapestry in which parts are silken, parts are tattered, and yet it all holds together. The question is: Is holding together sufficient for it to remain a democracy? Alternatively, do we need to ensure that democracy does not decay in tatters?

We need to do a great deal urgently to recover that liberal character of democracy envisaged in the Indian Constitution. The Indian political spectrum must widen its liberal space to push to the edges the intolerant rants of the far right and the far left. The founding fathers – Nehru, Ambedkar, Rajaji and the rest – had it relatively easy when they pronounced liberal principles and beliefs in the early days of India's democracy. They were more or less steeped in European liberal thought and were conversant with the tolerant tradition in Indian culture, starting with Gautam Buddha, through Emperors Ashoka and Harshavardhana and Akbar, through the leaders of the Bhakti movement, to contemporary apostles of tolerance and liberal values like Gandhi and Tagore. Democracy, however, shows a peculiar side in developing societies that are not sufficiently literate or fully conscious of civic virtues. The more it spreads, the more we need to strengthen it to help it maintain depth even as it expands horizontally. Both the politics and the educational system of a developing democracy have to expound liberalism with the intensity of religious indoctrination. Being a democracy that holds regular elections, changes governments and allows a degree of free speech is not enough to ensure long-term sustainability.

Contrary to a persisting Western assumption, India's democratic tradition was not a gift from the British; it grew in direct opposition to imperial rule. As Sumit Ganguly, Rabindranath Tagore Chair in Indian Cultures and Civilizations at Indiana University, said in an article in the April 2007 issue of the *Journal of Democracy*, the British did little or nothing to promote the growth of democratic institutions in India. Indian nationalists from the late nineteenth century onward, Ganguly added, successfully appropriated liberal-democratic principles from the United Kingdom and infused them into the Indian political context. As this was occurring, the British colonial regime was losing few opportunities to thwart or at least contain the growth of democratic sentiment and practice in India. 'The Indian nationalists justifiably claim that each step toward self-rule and democratic governance was the result of sustained and unrelenting political agitation against authoritarian colonial rule.'

By the time the nationalists could sit together in 1947 to draft a constitution for the new nation, they had become aware that the only system that could work for this diverse nation would be a secular democracy that promoted tolerance and pluralism to weld together a vast array of linguistic, religious and ethnic groups. It would have to be the non-Pakistan to prove the nationalists' point that an independent Indian people could live together in harmony while preserving their individual as well as group identities. Freedom of religion and the right to free speech and assembly were not seen as luxuries in a poor and developing nation. They were essential to India's survival as the world's most daring experiment in democratic nation building.

To ensure that survival, the quality of democracy must not be strained. In this multicultural, multi-religious, and multiethnic nation, the spirit of tolerance must be guarded, expanded and deepened at any cost to make India bloom. With economic liberalization, an aspiring, educated middle class has finally begun growing at a pace it could not during the so-called Licence-Permit Raj. After six decades of independence, there still are far too many living in utter misery in this land of ours, the largest number of poor living within a single national boundary anywhere. That reality will have to give way to a visibly just society in which disparities will exist but few will have to endure the destitution they have had to accept as their destiny. It is the growth of the middle class that will continue to reduce the numbers who live in abject poverty while an increasingly youthful desire for upward mobility will hopefully create an expanding constituency for a liberal society that is open to the world of ideas, is ready to live with dissent and remains deeply conscious of India's credibility as a truly tolerant democracy.

Eleven

IN CONCLUSION

The growth of a liberal society, and its necessary vehicle, a liberal polity, requires a steady and determined nurturing of a liberal mindset. A liberal mindset does not deny the reality of identities. It merely accepts the existence of a variety of possible identities. As Amartya Sen puts it in his book *Identity and Violence*, each one of us can have plural identities. I might be a Hindu by birth, an agnostic by choice, an Indian, a journalist, a father, a lover of cricket and soccer, and a liberal democrat. Which identity I adopt at which point of time in a day might depend on circumstances.

Those separate identities, in society as well as in each individual, require acceptance by other citizens of a republic even when any particular identity in one person might be provocatively challenging to another's deeply held belief or self-identity. That is the essence of the liberal mind, which often disagrees with another person's attitudes or beliefs but agrees that each individual's right to be different must be honoured. In other words, in a liberal democracy, every citizen must have equal rights despite differences in background, ability, race, class, caste, physical strength, mental ability and any other difference in capability or status.

That is a defining feature of the Constitution that our founding fathers drafted for the Republic of India. By guaranteeing an equal right to freedom of expression, assembly and religion to every citizen, they made a clear choice at the outset on our behalf. Those freedoms mark out a liberal democracy from all forms of illiberal societies.

Unfortunately, sixty years into the Indian experiment, far too many of our fellow citizens have yet to internalize the liberal mindset necessary to sustain the spirit of the Constitution. The effort to inculcate a liberal mind should normally be led by three branches of society: educational institutions, the media and the political leadership. Regrettably, they often fail in their task.

Take a widely respected educational institution like the University of Mumbai, for example. In October 2010, it decided to withdraw from a university reading list the book *Such A Long Journey* by the Indo-Canadian author Rohinton Mistry. In taking that decision the university capitulated to a demand by the Shiv Sena, which had been annoyed by negative references in the book to their supreme leader Bal Thackeray.

Mohan Rawale, a Sena official, said the book was full of 'very bad, very insulting words' about Thackeray. 'It is our culture that anything with insulting language should be deleted. Writers can't just write anything. They can't write wrong things,' he said to the press.

He is correct in asserting that a book that has been listed as recommended reading in a university list should not contain incorrect data. Indeed, he should challenge the author if stated facts are wrong. But he fails to see the crucial difference between fact and opinion. If a writer expresses a view – in this case a disparaging one about a person – he or she must have the full right to do so. Just as Rawale has a right to express his outrage, so must Mistry have the right to write what he feels about the Sena's leader. And the university must resolutely defend both rights.

The university, instead of defending this cornerstone of democratic liberalism and explaining publicly why it was doing it, simply capitulated to the Sena's demand. When a reputed institution like the University of Mumbai can sacrifice a principle so easily, students can hardly be expected to acquire a liberal mindset.

As for the media, in this day of talking heads on cable television, opinionating by star anchors with relentless aggression often threatens to push out balanced discussion and news stories. Several TV channels appear to have taken a leaf out of the book of the American cable channel Fox News, which claims to be 'fair and balanced' but is usually a mouthpiece for hard right-wing views that attract committed viewers.

Sometimes Indian TV talk shows verge on naked jingoism and take on the role of both prosecutor and judge when pursuing stories that can arouse high nationalist passion. Take for instance the uproar over a pronouncement by Arundhati Roy about Kashmir.

The novelist, as seems to be her habit, was expressing an extreme view. She asserted at a seminar in Srinagar in late October 2010: 'Kashmir has never been an integral part of India. It is a historical fact.' Now this is not the case and Roy, once again, was being characteristically provocative. Her reading and understanding of history were clearly selective. She seemed to be pandering to the contrarian view of a far left section of the intelligentsia and providing succour to anti-Indian forces across the border in Pakistan.

Was she doing anything blatantly unconstitutional? No. Did she have the right to say what she felt even if her reading of history was incorrect? Yes.

But some in the media, in an apparent effort to rouse popular passion and thereby gain eyeballs, went after her in a way that seemed to undermine that very right to freedom of expression that keeps the press in India independent. Mercifully, others in the media, in the right spirit of liberal debate, allowed Roy her freedom to say what she felt by publishing or broadcasting her views fairly and then criticizing her.

When the spirit of debate is eclipsed by tub-thumping nationalism in the media, our freedoms take a knock. Nationalist passion for India can easily sit with the Constitution's liberal spirit. Outright jingoism cannot.

At the same time, our political leaders, with a few honourable exceptions, seem to see themselves as our rulers rather than servers. They probably suffer from a feudal-imperial overhang that makes them conduct their lifestyles in a way that goes flatly against liberal concepts of equality, tolerance and public humility.

In the national capital and state capitals, in district headquarters and wherever else authority can be flaunted, senior politicians and state functionaries move about like they own the land. With their security factotums pushing everyone out of their way, they vie with one another to be included in a prized list of VVIPs who do not have to be cleared by the security at airports while normal citizens patiently wait in line.

A modicum of state-provided security is, of course, necessary for some people in the forefront of public life. They can be targets of terrorists and other militants simply for being public figures. But in India they, and often their families, are given taxpayer-paid protection to such an intrusive extent that the size and grade of a VIP's security detail, and the lights on top of their cars, become a visible determinant of status.

Perhaps most of us have not yet digested what it means to be a free citizen of a democratic republic. Deep in our minds many of us still think of anyone who has managed to move into a position of state-sanctioned authority as someone who has also earned a right to power in the manner of a monarch. But the way we accept and even exalt the notion of a VIP in this country should be embarrassing to citizens of a democracy.

Liberalism rests on three fundamental beliefs, the first of which is a desire for equality. In a post-industrial and post-democratic modern world, it is no longer possible to justify inequalities of rights and opportunities though inequality of outcome may be inevitable. The goal of public policy in a democracy must be to provide a more or less level playing field for citizens. Inequality serves narrow interests; striving for equality serves the interest of all. We may debate the extent and nature of facilitating equality but the fact of equality as a desired outcome is beyond dispute in a republic calling itself a liberal democracy.

A second essential feature of a liberal society is the protection of free expression. Historically, liberalism grew in opposition to societies that were closed to public opinion and were against new ideas. Debating ideas for social progress, growth and development is a crucial condition for improving the quality of life. Suppression of speech leads to closed, fearful minds. Freedom to say what we want lets ideas flower.

Third, any society claiming the liberal democratic mantle must thrive in diversity of thought and opinion, religion and ideology, race and ethnicity, culture and tradition. Although liberalism thrives on the triumph of reason, a liberal democracy must not deify reason to the extent that it refuses space and protection to persons of faith. A liberal society seeks to ensure freedom for religion as well as for the beliefs of the non-religious.

In India, we see far too many instances of even petty disputes erupting in violent outcomes. Anger over minor differences may be common in all societies. It is how that anger is managed and how frequently it bursts into open violence that a liberal democratic society has to watch. For instance, incidents of violent road rage in India, particularly in the capital region of New Delhi, are way more prevalent than in most major societies. A small accident of a car door being mistakenly opened to hit a passerby or a minor brush between two vehicles often leads to gunfire and death.

Perhaps people have lost or never developed any trust in public institutions – the police and the judicial system – and believe, in their collective subconscious selves, that they can expect neither speedy redress of grievances nor any quick and serious accountability for violent behaviour. India may have begun with every intention of being a democratic house that would resolve most of its myriad differences by providing an institutional framework of governance that the average citizen could rely upon. Today, however, India is a low-trust society. Its citizens do not believe sufficiently in the state's capacity, or willingness, to deliver reliable governance.

To reconstruct a tolerant India in which its people develop faith not only in the state's capacities but also in one another, we must strive to internalize the principle of live and let live in our collective minds. Without that core conviction, India might decay into an ungovernable mess. To avoid such an outcome, we must rediscover a space wide enough to rebuild and sustain a truly liberal society.

It is the kind of tolerant, accommodative society for which India's founding fathers laid the groundwork. They set the goals through crafting a fine Constitution. It is our responsibility to realize it as best as we can.

FOR FURTHER READING

Acharya, Shankar, and Rakesh Mohan (eds), *India's Economy: Performance and Challenges* (New Delhi: Oxford University Press [henceforth OUP], 2010).

Ahmad, Aziz, *Islamic Modernism in India and Pakistan 1857-1964* (London: OUP, 1967).

Andersen, Walter K., and Shridhar D. Damle, *The Brotherhood in Saffron: The Rashtriya Swayamsevak Sangh and Hindu Revivalism* (Boulder, California: Westview, 1987).

Aslan, Reza, *No god but God: The Origins, Evolution, and Future of Islam* (New York: Random House Trade Paperbacks, 2006).

Austin, Granville, *Working a Democratic Constitution: A History of the Indian Experience* (Oxford: OUP, 2003).

Bhalla, Surjit S., *Imagine There's No Country: Poverty, Inequality, and Growth in the Era of Globalization* (Washington, DC: Institute for International Economics, 2002).

Bhargava, Rajeev (ed.), *Secularism and Its Critics* (New Delhi: OUP, 1999).

Brass, Paul R., *The Politics of India since Independence* (Cambridge: Cambridge University Press, 1990).

Chandhoke, Neera, *Beyond Secularism: The Rights of Religious Minorities* (New Delhi: OUP, 2002).

Chatterjee, Partha, 'Secularism and Tolerance', in Rajeev Bhargava (ed.), *Secularism and Its Critics* (New Delhi: OUP, 1999).

Dawkins, Richard, *The God Delusion* (London: Bantam, 2006).

Diamond, Larry, and Marc F. Plattner, *Capitalism, Socialism, and Democracy Revisited* (Baltimore: Johns Hopkins University Press, 1993).

Dumont, Louis, *Religion, Politics and History in India: Collected Papers in Indian Sociology* [Ecole Pratique Des Hautes Études, Sorbonne. 6. Section] (The Hague: Mouton, 1970).

Engineer, Asghar Ali, *Babri Masjid-Ramjanambhumi Controversy* (New Delhi: Ajanta Publications, 1990).

Ferris, Timothy, *The Science of Liberty: Democracy, Reason, and the Laws of Nature* (New York: Harper 2010).

Ganguly, Sumit, Larry Diamond, and Marc F. Plattner, *The State of India's Democracy* (Baltimore: Johns Hopkins University Press, 2007).

Gopal, Sarvepalli, *Anatomy of a Confrontation: the Babri Masjid-Ramjanmabhumi Issue* (New Delhi: Viking Penguin, 1991).

—— (ed.), *Jawaharlal Nehru: An Anthology* (New Delhi: OUP, 1980).

——*The Political Abuse of History* (New Delhi: Centre for Historical Studies, Jawaharlal Nehru University, 1989).

Guha, Ramachandra, *India after Gandhi: The History of the World's Largest Democracy* (New Delhi: Picador, 2007).

Harris, Sam, *The End of Faith: Religion, Terror, and the Future of Reason* (New York: W.W. Norton, 2004).

Hitchens, Christopher, *God Is Not Great: How Religion Poisons Everything* (New York: Hachette Book Group, 2007).

Iyer, Raghavan (ed.), *The Essential Writings of Mahatma Gandhi* (New Delhi: OUP, 2005).

Jalan, Bimal, *The Indian Economy: Problems and Prospects* (New Delhi: Viking Penguin, 1992).

Jayal, Niraja Gopal, and Pratap Bhanu Mehta, *The Oxford Companion to Politics in India* (New Delhi: OUP, 2010).

Kakar, Sudhir, *Shamans, Mystics, and Doctors: A Psychological Inquiry into India and Its Healing Traditions* (New York: Alfred A. Knopf, 1982).

Lewis, Bernard, *The Crisis of Islam: Holy War and Unholy Terror* (New York: Random House, 2004).

———, *What Went Wrong?: Western Impact and Middle Eastern Response* (Oxford: OUP, 2002).

Madan, T. N., 'Secularism in Its Place', in Rajeev Bhargava (ed.), *Secularism and Its Critics* (New Delhi: OUP, 1999).

Mehta, Pratap Bhanu. 'On The Possibility of Religious Pluralism', in Thomas Banchoff (ed.), *Challenges of Religious Pluralism in a Global Era* (Oxford: OUP, 2008).

Naipaul, V. S., *An Area of Darkness* (London: Penguin, 1968).

———, *India: A Wounded Civilization* (Harmondsworth: Penguin, 1979).

Nandy, Ashis, 'Hinduism versus Hindutva', *The Times of India*, 18 February 1991.

———, *The Intimate Enemy: Loss and Recovery of Self Under Colonialism* (New Delhi: OUP, 1992).

———, 'The Politics of Secularism and the Recovery of Religious Tolerance', in Veena Das (ed.), *Mirrors of Violence: Communities, Riots and Survivors in South Asia* (New Delhi: OUP, 1990), pp. 69-93.

Nehru, Jawaharlal. *The Discovery of India* (New Delhi: OUP, 1989).

Nussbaum, Martha C., *The Clash Within: Democracy, Religious*

Violence, and India's Future (New Delhi: Permanent Black, 2007).

Pandey, Gyanendra, *The Construction of Communalism in Colonial North India* (New Delhi: OUP, 1990).

Parekh, Bhikhu, *Colonialism, Tradition, Reform: An Analysis of Gandhi's Political Discourse* (New Delhi: Sage, 1989).

Radhakrishnan, Sarvepalli, *The Hindu View of Life* (New York: Macmillan, 1957).

Raychaudhuri, Tapan, 'Swami Vivekananda's Construction of Hinduism', in William Radice (ed.), *Swami Vivekananda and the Modernization of Hinduism* (New Delhi: OUP, 1998).

Rudolph, Lloyd I., and Susanne H. Rudolph, *In Pursuit of Lakshmi: The Political Economy of the Indian State* (Bombay: Orient Longman, 1987).

———,*The Modernity of Tradition: Political Development in India* (Chicago: University of Chicago Press, 1967).

Said, Edward W., *Orientalism* (New York: Fontana, 1979).

Savarkar, V. D., *Hindutva* (Poona: S.R. Date, 1942).

Sen, Amartya, *Identity and Violence: The Illusion of Destiny* (London: Allen Lane, 2006).

———, *The Argumentative Indian: Writings on Indian History, Culture and Identity* (London: Allen Lane, 2005).

Sen, K. M., *Hinduism* (London: Penguin, 1961).

Sen, Ronojoy, *Articles of Faith: Religion, Secularism, and the Indian Supreme Court* (New Delhi: OUP, 2010).

Shourie, Arun, *A Secular Agenda: For Saving Our Country, for Welding It* (New Delhi: ASA Publications, 1993).

Starr, Paul, *Freedom's Power: the True Force of Liberalism* (New York: Basic, 2007).

Thapar, Romila, 'Is Secularism Alien to Indian Civilization', in T.N. Srinivasan (ed.), *The Future of Secularism* (Oxford: OUP, 2007).

Thapar, Romila, Harbans Mukhia, and Bipan Chandra, *Communalism and the Writing of Indian History* (Delhi: People's Publishing House, 1969).

Wolfe, Alan, *The Future of Liberalism* (New York: Alfred A. Knopf, 2009).

INDEX

ABOUT THE AUTHOR

Gautam Adhikari is a journalist, writer and television commentator. He has been executive editor, editorial page editor, foreign correspondent and editorial adviser of *The Times of India* and dean of the Times School of Journalism. In 2005, Adhikari was the founding editor of *DNA* (*Daily News & Analysis*), Mumbai.

Currently a FICCI-EWC Fellow at the East West Center in Washington, DC, Adhikari has been resident fellow and adjunct lecturer in public policy at the Shorenstein Center for Press/Politics at Harvard University (1987-89), and AT&T Scholar (1994) and J.B. & Maurice C. Shapiro Fellow (1997-98) at George Washington University.

He was senior resident fellow at the International Forum for Democratic Studies in Washington and project director of the World Movement for Democracy and the Asian Center for Democratic Governance (1998-2003).